MW01147260

IMPERIALISM AND WORLD ECONOMY

IMPERIALISM AND
WORLD ECONOMY

By NIKOLAI BUKHARIN
Author of Historical Materialism, The Economic
Theory of the Leisure Class, etc.

With an introduction by
V. I. LENIN

LONDON
MARTIN LAWRENCE LIMITED

All Rights Reserved

———

Printed in the United States of America

This book is composed and printed by union labor.

CONTENTS

PART I

WORLD ECONOMY AND THE PROCESS OF INTERNATIONALISATION OF CAPITAL

CHAPTER I

1. Imperialism as a problem of world economy. 2. International division of labour as a case of social division of labour. 3. Natural and social prerequisites for international division of labour. 4. International exchange of commodities as a necessary and regular process. 5. The world market of commodities. 6. The world market of money capital. 7. World economy as a system of production relations. 8. Various forms of establishing production relations. 9. Social economy in general and world economy (subject of economic activity).

CHAPTER II

1. Extensive and intensive growth of world economy. 2. Growth of productive forces of world economy; technique. 3. Production of coal, iron ore, cast iron, copper, gold. 4. Production of other goods. 5. Transport industry: railroads, ocean transport. Telegraph and ocean cables. 6. Growth of foreign trade. 7. Migration. 8. Movement of capital (capital export) and its forms. 9. Participation in, and financing of, foreign enterprises (activities of industrial enterprises and banks).

CHAPTER III

1. Anarchic structure of world economy. 2. International syndicates and cartels. 3. International trusts. 4. International bank syndicates. 5. Nature of international, purely capitalist organisations. 6. Internationalisation of economic life and internationalisation of capitalist interests.

PART II

WORLD ECONOMY AND THE PROCESS OF NATIONALISATION OF CAPITAL

CHAPTER IV

CHAPTER V

CHAPTER VI

CHAPTER VII

CHAPTER VIII

CHAPTER XIII

CHAPTER XIV

CHAPTER XV

INTRODUCTION *

By V. I. LENIN

THE importance and timeliness of the topic treated in the work of N. I. Bukharin require no particular elucidation. The problem of imperialism is not only a most essential one, but, we may say, it is the most essential problem in that realm of economic science which examines the changing forms of capitalism in recent times. Every one interested not only in economics but in any sphere of present-day social life must acquaint himself with the facts relating to this problem, as presented by the author in such detail on the basis of the latest available data. Needless to say that there can be no concrete historical analysis of the present war, if that analysis does not have for its basis a full understanding of the nature of imperialism, both from its economic and political aspects. Without this, it is impossible to approach an understanding of the economic and diplomatic situation of the last decades, and without such an understanding, it is ridiculous even to speak of forming a correct view on the war. From the point of view of Marxism, which most clearly expresses the requirements of modern science in general, one can only smile at the "scientific" value of a method which consists in culling from diplomatic "documents" or from daily political events only such isolated facts as would be pleasant and convenient for the ruling classes of one country, and parading this as a historic analysis of the war. Such is the case, for instance, with Plekhanov, who parted ways with Marxism altogether when, instead of analysing the fundamental characteristics and tendencies of imperialism as a system of the economic relations of modern highly developed, mature, and over-ripe capitalism, he started angling after bits of facts to please the Purishkeviches and the Milyukovs. Under such conditions the scientific concept of imperialism is

* This introduction was originally signed by Lenin with the pseudonym V. Ilyin.—Ed.

9

reduced to the level of a cuss-word addressed to the immediate
competitors, rivals, and opponents of the two above-mentioned
Russian imperialists, whose class basis is entirely identical
with that of their foreign rivals and opponents.   In these times
of forsaken words, renounced principles, overthrown world conceptions, abandoned resolutions and solemn promises, one must
not be surprised at that.

The scientific significance of N. I. Bukharin's work consists
particularly in this, that he examines the fundamental facts of
world economy relating to imperialism as a whole, as a definite
stage in the growth of most highly developed capitalism.   There
had been an epoch of a comparatively "peaceful capitalism,"
when it had overcome feudalism in the advanced countries of
Europe and was in a position to develop comparatively tran-
quilly and harmoniously, "peacefully" spreading over tremendous areas of still unoccupied lands, and of countries not yet
finally drawn into the capitalist vortex.   Of course, even in
that epoch, marked approximately by the years 1871 and 1914,
" peaceful" capitalism created conditions of life that were very
far from being really peaceful both in the military and in a
general class sense.   For nine-tenths of the population of the
advanced countries, for hundreds of millions of peoples in the
colonies and in the backward countries this epoch was not one
of "peace" but of oppression, tortures, horrors that seemed the
more terrifying since they appeared to be without end.   This
epoch has gone forever.   It has been followed by a new epoch,
comparatively more impetuous, full of abrupt changes, catastrophes, conflicts, an epoch that no longer appears to the
toiling masses as horror without end but is an end full of
horrors.

It is highly important to have in mind that this change was
caused by nothing but the direct development, growth, continuation of the deep-seated and fundamental tendencies of
capitalism and production of commodities in general.   The
growth of commodity exchange, the growth of large-scale production are fundamental tendencies observable for centuries
throughout the whole world.   At a certain stage in the development of exchange, at a certain stage in the growth of large-
scale production, namely, at the stage that was reached ap-

proximately at the end of the nineteenth and the beginning of the twentieth centuries, commodity exchange had created such an internationalisation of economic relations, and such an internationalisation of capital, accompanied by such a vast increase in large-scale production, that free competition began to be replaced by monopoly. The prevailing types were no longer enterprises freely competing inside the country and through intercourse between countries, but monopoly alliances of entrepreneurs, trusts. The typical ruler of the world became finance capital, a power that is peculiarly mobile and flexible, peculiarly intertwined at home and internationally, peculiarly devoid of individuality and divorced from the immediate processes of production, peculiarly easy to concentrate, a power that has already made peculiarly large strides on the road of concentration, so that literally several hundred billionaires and millionaires hold in their hands the fate of the whole world.

Reasoning theoretically and in the abstract, one may arrive at the conclusion reached by Kautsky (who, like many others, has parted ways with Marxism, but in a different manner), that the time is not far off when those magnates of capital will unite into one world trust which would replace the rivalries and the struggle of nationally limited finance capital by an internationally united finance capital. Such a conclusion, however, is just as abstract, simplified, and incorrect as an analogous conclusion, arrived at by our "Struveists" and "Economists" of the nineties of the last century. The latter, proceeding from the progressive nature of capitalism, from its inevitability, from its final victory in Russia, at times became apologetic (worshipping capital, making peace agreements with it, praising it instead of fighting it); at times became non-political (*i. e.*, rejected politics, or the importance of politics, denied the probability of general political convulsions, etc., this being the favourite error of the "Economists"); at times even preached "strike" pure and simple ("general strike" to them was the apotheosis of the strike movement; it was elevated to a position where other forms of the movement are forgotten or ignored; it was a *salto mortale* from capitalism to its destruction by strikes alone). There are indications that the undisputed progressiveness of capitalism, compared with the semi-philistine "paradise" of free competition, and the inevitability of imperialism with its final victory over "peaceful" capital in the advanced countries of the world, may at present lead to political and non-political errors and misadventures no less numerous or varied.

Particularly as regards Kautsky, his open break with Marxism has led him, not to reject or forget politics, nor to skim over the numerous and varied political conflicts, convulsions and transformations that particularly characterise the imperialist epoch; nor to become an apologist of imperialism; but to *dream about a "peaceful capitalism."* "Peaceful" capitalism has been replaced by unpeaceful, militant, catastrophic imperialism. This Kautsky is compelled to admit, for he admitted it as early as 1909 in a special work[1] in which he drew sound conclusions as a Marxist for the last time. If it is thus impossible simply, directly, and bluntly to dream of going from imperialism back to "peaceful" capitalism, is it not possible to give those essentially petty-bourgeois dreams the appearance of innocent contemplations regarding "peaceful" ultra-imperialism? If the name of ultra-imperialism is given to an international unification of national (or, more correctly, state-bound) imperialisms which "would be able" to eliminate the most unpleasant, the most disturbing and distasteful conflicts such as wars, political convulsions, etc., which the petty bourgeois is so much afraid of, then why not turn away from the present epoch of imperialism that has already arrived—the epoch that stares one in the face, that is full of all sorts of conflicts and catastrophes? Why not turn to innocent dreams of a comparatively peaceful, comparatively conflictless, comparatively non-catastrophic ultra-imperialism? And why not wave aside the "exacting" tasks that have been posed by the epoch of imperialism now ruling in Europe? Why not turn instead of dreaming that this epoch will perhaps soon be over, that perhaps it will be followed by a comparatively "peaceful" epoch of ultra-imperialism which demands no such "sharp" tactics? Kautsky says directly that at any rate "such a new [ultra-imperialist] phase of capitalism is thinkable. Whether,

[1] This is his pamphlet, *Der Weg zur Macht* [*The Road to Power*].

however, it can be realised, to answer this question we have not yet sufficient data." (*Neue Zeit*, April 30, 1915, p. 144.) [1]

In this tendency to evade the imperialism that is here and to pass in dreams to an epoch of "ultra-imperialism," of which we do not even know whether it is realisable, there is not a grain of Marxism. In this reasoning Marxism is admitted for that "new phase of capitalism," the realisability of which its inventor himself fails to vouch for, whereas for the present, the existing phase of capitalism, he offers us not Marxism, but a petty-bourgeois and deeply reactionary tendency to soften contradictions. There was a time when Kautsky promised to be a Marxist in the coming restless and catastrophic epoch, which he was compelled to foresee and definitely recognise when writing his work in 1909 about the coming war. Now, when it has become absolutely clear that that epoch has arrived, Kautsky again only promises to be a Marxist in the coming epoch of ultra-imperialism, of which he does not know whether it will arrive! In other words, we have any number of his promises to be a Marxist some time in another epoch, not under present conditions, not at this moment. For to-morrow we have Marxism on credit, Marxism as a promise, Marxism deferred. For to-day we have a petty-bourgeois opportunist theory—and not only a theory—of softening contradictions. It is something like the internationalism for export prevailing in our days among ardent—ever so ardent!—internationalists and Marxists who sympathise with every expression of internationalism in the enemy's camp, anywhere but not at home, not among their allies; who sympathise with democracy as long as it remains a promise of their allies; who sympathise with the "self-determination of nations" but not of those that are dependent upon the nation honoured by the membership of the sympathiser—in a word, this is one of the thousand and one varieties of hypocrisy prevailing in our times.

Can one, however, deny that in the abstract a new phase of capitalism to follow imperialism, namely, a phase of ultra-imperialism, is "thinkable"? No. In the abstract one can think of such a phase. In practice, however, he who denies

---

[1] This passage is taken from Kautsky's article entitled "Zwei Schritte zum Umlernen", (Two Steps to Unlearn), *Neue Zeit*, No. 5, 1915.

the sharp tasks of to-day in the name of dreams about soft tasks of the future becomes an opportunist. Theoretically it means to fail to base oneself on the developments now going on in real life, to detach oneself from them in the name of dreams. There is no doubt that the development is going *in the direction* of a single world trust that will swallow up all enterprises and all states without exception. But the development in this direction is proceeding under such stress, with such a tempo, with such contradictions, conflicts, and convulsions—not only economical, but also political, national, etc., etc.—that before a single world trust will be reached, before the respective national finance capitals will have formed a world union of "ultra-imperialism," imperialism will inevitably explode, capitalism will turn into its opposite.

December, 1915.

PREFACE

THE essay to which we here call the attention of the reader represents an elaboration of an article published abroad in the almanac *Communist*. In due time, about two years ago, the manuscript was shipped from abroad to Russia. First it was subjected to a raid by the military censor, then it was mistakenly transmitted to the wrong publisher. After the Revolution of February-March, 1917, the manuscript was "found." It was supposed to see the light of day in July, but the intelligence men and the cadets who raided our party printing plant, also took care of my manuscript. Much later it was rescued in a mutilated form; a large and highly valuable introduction by Comrade Lenin, to whom I here pay the debt of deep gratitude, was missing.[1]

Due to the fact that the composition of this work dates back two years, the statistical figures are, naturally, antiquated, especially those relating to the effects of the war.

Unfortunately, I have had no occasion as yet to revise the manuscript and to furnish it with fresh statistical material. I have only re-written the missing pages and added the last chapter, which could not have appeared under the censor's rule.

The manuscript was written at a time when Socialism, crucified by capital and the "Socialist" traitors, was suffering the greatest possible humiliations. Soon after he had sent it to Russia, the author had ample time to ponder over revolutionary perspectives in the Swedish king's prison.

This preface is written at a moment when revolutionary Socialism has achieved its greatest victory in Russia.

It is the most ardent wish of the author that this book should soon be transformed from a weapon against imperialism into an historic document relegated to the archives.

November 25, 1917.

[1] The manuscript of the introduction, included in the present volume, was subsequently found and first published in the *Pravda*, January 21, 1927.—*Ed.*

PART I

WORLD ECONOMY AND THE PROCESS OF
INTERNATIONALISATION OF CAPITAL

CHAPTER I

World Economy Defined

1. IMPERIALISM AS A PROBLEM OF WORLD ECONOMY. 2. INTER-
NATIONAL DIVISION OF LABOUR AS A CASE OF SOCIAL DIVISION OF
LABOUR. 3. NATURAL AND SOCIAL PREREQUISITES FOR INTERNA-
TIONAL DIVISION OF LABOUR. 4. INTERNATIONAL EXCHANGE OF
COMMODITIES AS A NECESSARY AND REGULAR PROCESS. 5. THE
WORLD MARKET OF COMMODITIES. 6. THE WORLD MARKET OF
MONEY CAPITAL. 7. WORLD ECONOMY AS A SYSTEM OF PRODUCTION
RELATIONS. 8. VARIOUS FORMS OF ESTABLISHING PRODUCTION RELA-
TIONS. 9. SOCIAL ECONOMY IN GENERAL AND WORLD ECONOMY
(SUBJECT OF ECONOMIC ACTIVITY).

THE struggle between "national" states, which is nothing
but the struggle between the respective groups of the bourgeoisie, is not suspended in the air. One cannot picture this
gigantic conflict as the conflict of two bodies in a vacuum.
On the contrary, the very conflict is conditioned by the special medium in which the "national economic organisms" live
and grow. The latter, however, have long ceased being a
secluded whole, an "isolated economy" à la Fichte or Thünen.
On the contrary, they are only parts of a much larger sphere,
namely, *world economy*. Just as every individual enterprise
is part of the "national" economy, so every one of these "national economies" is included in the system of world economy.
This is why the struggle between modern "national economic
bodies" must be regarded first of all as the struggle of various
competing parts of world economy—just as we consider the
struggle of individual enterprises to be one of the phenomena
of socio-economic life. Thus the problem of studying imperialism, its economic characteristics, and its future, reduces itself

to the problem of analysing the tendencies in the development of world economy, and of the probable changes in its inner structure. Before we approach this problem, however, we must, first of all, agree as to what we understand by the expression "world economy."

The basis of social life is the production of material goods. In modern society, which produces not products as such but commodities, *i.e.*, products destined for exchange, the process of the exchange of various products expresses the division of labour between the economic units that produce those commodities. Such division of labour, in contradistinction to the division of labour within the framework of a single enterprise, is termed by Marx the social division of labour. Social division of labour can obviously assume various forms; there may be, for instance, division of labour between various enterprises within a country; or there may be division of labour between various branches of production; there may also be division of labour between such large subdivisions of the entire economic life as, for instance, industry and agriculture; and there may be division of labour between countries that represent separate economic systems inside of the general system, etc.

It is possible to propose various divisions, to advance more than one basis for the classification of economic forms, depending upon the aims pursued by the investigation. What is important for us in this connection is the fact that, alongside of other forms of social division of labour, there exists a division of labour between "national economies," between various countries, a division of labour which oversteps the boundaries of the "national economy,"—an international division of labour.

There exist two kinds of prerequisites for an international division of labour: natural prerequisites conditioned by the differences of the natural medium in which the various "production organisms" live, and prerequisites of a social nature conditioned by the differences in the cultural level, the economic structure, and the development of productive forces in the various countries.

Let us start with the former.

Different communities discover in their natural environment different means for production and subsistence. Consequently their methods of production, modes of life, and products, are different. It is owing to the existence of these spontaneously developed differences that, when communities come into contact, there occurs an exchange of their several products one for another, so that these products gradually become transformed into commodities. Exchange does not create the difference between the spheres of production; it brings the differing spheres of production into relation one with another, and thus transforms them into more or less interdependent branches of a social collective production.[1]

This difference in the spheres of production results here from the differences in the natural conditions of production. It is not difficult to find numerous illustrations for this assertion. Let us, for example, take the vegetable kingdom.

Coffee can be produced only under certain climatic conditions. It is grown mainly in Brazil, partly in Central America, to a much lesser degree in Africa (Abyssinia, British Central Africa, German East Africa), and in Asia (Dutch India, British India, Arabia, Malakka). Cocoa can be produced only in tropical countries. Rubber, a product playing a very large part in modern production, also requires certain climatic conditions, and its production is limited to a few countries (Brazil, Ecuador, Peru, Bolivia, Guiana, etc.). Cotton, a product occupying the first rank among all fibrous plants due to its importance in economic life is produced in the United States, India, Egypt, China, Asia Minor, and the Russian Central Asia territories. Jute, which takes the second place, is exported from one country only, namely, from India. If we take the production of minerals, we find the same picture, since we deal here to a certain extent with what is known as the "natural resources" of a country. Coal, for instance, is exported from countries with large coal deposits (England, Germany, United States, Austria, etc.); kerosene is produced in countries having an abundance of oil (United States, the Caucasus, Holland, India, Roumania, Galicia); iron ore is extracted in Spain, Sweden, France, Algeria, Newfoundland,

[1] Karl Marx: *Capital*, Vol. I (English translation by Eden and Cedar Paul), p. 371. In the following examples we do not cite the countries where a given article is merely produced; we cite only those countries from which it is exported.

Cuba, etc.; manganese ore is to be found mainly in the Caucasus and Southern Russia, India, and Brazil; copper deposits are in abundance mostly in Spain, Japan, British South Africa, German Southwest Africa, Australia, Canada, United States, Mexico, Chile, and Bolivia.

Important as the natural differences in the conditions of production may be, they recede more and more into the background compared with differences that are the outcome of the uneven development of productive forces in the various countries.

It must be emphasised that *natural conditions* are only of relative importance as regards production relations, as well as commerce and transport, *i.e.*, their negative or positive significance depends to a high degree upon the cultural level of man. While natural conditions . . . (measured by the human yardstick of time and space) may be regarded as constant entities, the cultural level of man is a changing entity, and no matter how important the differences in the natural conditions of a country may be for production and transport, the cultural differences are certainly as important, and only the combined action of both forces produces the phenomena of economic life.[1]

Coal deposits, for instance, may be "dead capital" in the absence of technical and economic prerequisites for their extraction. On the other hand, mountains formerly obstructing communication, swamps making production difficult, and the like, lose their negative significance in a country with a highly developed technique (tunnels, irrigation works, etc.).   Still more important for us is the circumstance that the unequal development of productive forces creates different economic types and different production spheres, thus increasing the scope of international social division of labour.   We have in mind the difference between industrial countries importing agricultural products and exporting manufactured goods, and agrarian countries exporting the products of agricultural production and importing the products of industry.

The foundation of all highly developed divisions of labour that are brought about by the exchange of commodities is the cleavage be-

[1] Ernst Friedrich: *Geographie des Welthandels und Weltverkehrs*, Jena, 1911, p. 7.

tween town and country. We may say that the whole economic history of society is summarised in the development of this cleavage. . . .[1]

The cleavage between "town and country," as well as the "development of this cleavage," formerly confined to one country only, are now being reproduced on a tremendously enlarged basis. Viewed from this standpoint, entire countries appear to-day as "towns," namely, the industrial countries, whereas entire agrarian territories appear to be "country." International division of labour coincides here with the division of labour between the two largest branches of social production as a whole, between industry and agriculture, thus appearing as the so-called "general division of labour."[2] This can be clearly realised by comparing the localities where the products of industry and agriculture are produced. Wheat is mainly produced in Canada, in the agrarian sections of the United States, in Argentina, Australia, and Western India, in Russia, Roumania, Bulgaria, Serbia, Hungary. Rye is produced mainly in Russia. Meat is delivered by Australia and New Zealand, the United States (agrarian sections), Canada (which specialises in large-scale production of meat), Argentina, Denmark, Holland, etc. Live stock is exported mainly from the agrarian countries of Europe into the industrial countries. The centres of European production of live stock are Hungary, Holland, Denmark, Spain, Portugal, Russia, and the Balkan countries. Timber is furnished by Sweden, Finland, Norway, Northern Russia, partly by some sections of former Austria-Hungary; the export of timber from Canada has also begun to increase.

If, then, we were to single out the countries that export manufactured goods, they would prove to be the most developed industrial countries of the world. Cotton fabrics are primarily placed upon the market by Great Britain; then fol-

[1] Karl Marx, l. c., pp. 371-372.

[2] "If we keep labour alone in view, we can describe the division of social production into its main departments, such as agriculture, industry, etc., as the division of labour in general; and we can describe the splitting up of these departments of production into varieties and subvarieties as the division of labour in particular; while, last of all, we can describe the division of labour within the workshop as the division of labour in detail." (Karl Marx, l. c., p. 370.)

low Germany, France, Italy, Belgium, and in the Western Hemisphere, the United States. Woolen goods are produced for the world market by Great Britain, France, Germany, Austria, Belgium, etc. Iron and steel products are manufactured mainly by Great Britain, Germany, and the United States, the three countries that have attained the highest level of industrialism; the second place in this respect is occupied by a group consisting of Belgium, France, and Austria-Hungary. Chemicals are produced by Germany, which in this respect occupies the first place, then by England, the United States, France, Belgium, and Switzerland.[1]

We thus observe a peculiar distribution of the productive forces of world capitalism. The main subdivisions of social labour are separated by the line that divides two types of countries; social labour proves to be divided on an international scale.

International division of labour finds its expression in international exchange.

Inasmuch as the producers do not come into social contact until they exchange their labour products, the specifically social character of their individual labour does not manifest itself until exchange takes place. In other words, the labour of individuals becomes an effective part of the aggregate of social labour solely in virtue of the relations which the process of exchange establishes between the labour products and consequently between the producers.[2]

The social labour of the world as a whole is divided among the various countries; the labour of every individual country becomes part of that world social labour through the exchange that takes place on an international scale. This interdependence of countries brought about by the process of exchange is by no means an accident; it is a necessary condition for continued social growth. International exchange thereby turns into a process of socio-economic life governed by definite laws. The socio-economic life of the world would be entirely disorganised if America or Australia ceased exporting their wheat and live stock; England and Belgium, their coal; Russia, grain and raw materials; Germany, its machines and the products

[1] E. Friedrich, l. c.
[2] Karl Marx: *Capital*, Vol. I, p. 46.

of the chemical industry; India, Egypt, and the United States, cotton, etc. On the other hand, the countries that export the products of agriculture would be doomed to destruction were the markets for those products suddenly closed. This is particularly evident as regards the so-called "mono-cultural" countries, *i.e.*, such as produce one single product (coffee in Brazil, cotton in Egypt, etc.). How indispensable international exchange is at present for the normal process of economic life may be seen from the following examples. During the first third of the nineteenth century England imported only 2.5 per cent of foodstuffs needed for its population. Now it imports about 50 per cent of its grain (of wheat even as much as 80 per cent), 50 per cent of its meat, 70 per cent of its butter, 50 per cent of its cheese, etc.[1]

According to Lexis' calculations, the foreign market has for the Belgian manufacturers a significance equal to that of the home market; in England, the home market hardly absorbs double the amount of manufactured goods, metals, and coal that is to be exported; in Germany the home market exceeds the foreign market 4 to 4.5 times.[2]

According to Ballod, England imports between three-fourths and four-fifths of all the necessary wheat, and between 40 and 50 per cent of its meat; Germany imports 24 to 30 per cent of its breadstuffs, about 60 per cent of its fodder, and 5 to 10 per cent of its meat.[3]

The number of examples could be increased indefinitely. One thing is clear from the above. There is a regular market connection, through the process of exchange, between numberless individual economies scattered over the most diverse geographical areas. Thus, world division of labour and international exchange presuppose the existence of a *world market and world prices*. The level of prices is, generally speaking, not determined by production costs as is the case in local or "national" production. To a very large extent "national" and local differences are levelled out in the general resultant of world prices which, in their turn, exert pressure on individual

[1] Bernhard Harms: *Volkswirtschaft und Weltwirtschaft*, Jena, 1912, p. 176.
[2] H. Sieveking: *Auswärtige Handelspolitik*, Leipzig, 1910, p. 127.
[3] Karl Ballod: *Grundriss der Statistik*, Berlin, 1913, p. 118 ff.

producers, individual countries, individual territories. This is particularly manifest in the case of such commodities as coal and iron, wheat and cotton, coffee and wool, meat and sugar. The production of grains may serve as an example. Conditions of grain production differ widely in the various countries, whereas the price deviations are by no means as great.

PRICE PER THOUSAND KILOGRAMMES (IN MARKS)
BETWEEN 1901 AND 1908:

Markets	Rye	Wheat	Oats
Vienna	146	168	149
Paris	132	183	...
London	...	139	138
New York	...	141	...
Germany	155	183	163 [1]

The conditions of wheat production in England and America are widely different. Yet wheat prices are almost the same at the London and New York markets (139 and 141 marks per kilogramme respectively). This is due to the fact that an immense stream of American wheat is continually pouring over the Atlantic Ocean into England and Western Europe in general.

The formation and the movement of these world prices may be seen most clearly in the commodity exchanges of the largest cities of the world: London, New York, Berlin, where world prices are registered daily, information comes in from every corner of the world and thus world demand and world supply are being taken into account.

International exchange of commodities is based on the international division of labour. We must not think, however, that it takes place only within the limits set by the latter. Countries mutually exchange not only different products, but even products of the same kind. A, for instance, may export into B not only such products as are not produced in B, or produced in a very small quantity; it may export its commodities into B to compete with local production. In such cases, international exchange has its basis, not in division of labour which presupposes ·the production of different use-values, but solely

[1] J. Conrad: "Getreidenpreise," in *Handwörterbuch der Staatswissenschaften.*

in different levels of production-costs, in values having various scales in the various countries, but reduced, through international exchange, to socially indispensable labour on a world scale.[1]

How closely the various countries have become knitted by the process of the exchange of commodities may be seen from the economy in means of payment, *i.e.*, economy in the transportation of gold bullion.

If, on the one hand, we were to add the export of bullion of a certain country to its import, on the other hand the export of commodities of a country to its import, it would be seen that the value of bullion shipments was never more than 5 per cent of the value of commodity shipments. Besides, we must not forget that the trade balance of a country is only a portion of its balance of payments.[2]

Just as there is formed a world commodity market in the sphere of commodity exchange, so there is formed a world market of money capital. This is expressed in an international equalisation of the interest and discount rates. Thus "the element of finance also shows a tendency to aid in substituting for the market conditions of an individual country, the world market conditions (*Weltkonjunktur*).[3]

The example of the commodity market shows that behind the market relations there are hidden production relations. Any connection between producers who meet in the process of exchange presupposes the individual labours of the producers having already become elements of the combined labour of a social whole. Thus production is hidden behind exchange, production relations are hidden behind exchange relations, the interrelation of producers is hidden behind the interrelation of commodities. Where connections established through the process of exchange are not of an accidental nature, we have a stable system of production relations which forms the economic structure of society. Thus we may define world economy

[1] It is true that in the first case the difference in production costs is also of importance. However, it expresses the fact that *different* goods are produced, whereas in the second case no such fact is expressed.

[2] Julius Wolf: *Das internationale Zahlungswesen*, Leipzig, 1913, p. 62, (in *Veröffentlichungen des mitteleuropäischen Wirtschaftsvereins in Deutschland*, Heft XIV).

[3] Weill: *Die Solidarität der Geldmärkte*, Frankfurt a. M., 1903, p. 115.

as *a system of production relations and, correspondingly, of exchange relations on a world scale*. One must not assume, however, that production relations are established solely in the process of commodity exchange. "Whenever human beings work for one another *in any way*, their labour acquires a social form" [1] (*Italics ours.—N.B.*); in other words, whatever the form of connections established between producers, whether directly or indirectly, once a connection has been established and has acquired a stable character, we may speak of a system of production relations, *i.e.*, of the growth (or formation) of a social economy. It thus appears that commodity exchange is one of the most primitive forms of expressing production relations. Present-day highly complicated economic life knows a great variety of forms behind which production relations are hidden. When, for instance, the shares of an American enterprise are bought at the Berlin stock exchange, production relations are thereby established between the German capitalist and the American worker. When a Russian city obtains a loan from London capitalists and pays interest on the loan, then this is what happens: part of the surplus value expressing the relation that exists between the English worker and the English capitalist is transferred to the municipal government of a Russian city; the latter, in paying interest, gives away part of the surplus value received by the bourgeoisie of that city and expressing the production relations existing between the Russian worker and the Russian capitalist. Thus connections are established both between the workers and the capitalists of two countries. Of particular significance is the rôle of the ever growing movement of money capital, which we have noted above. A number of other forms of economic relations may be observed, like emigration and immigration; migration of the labour power; partial transfer of the wages of immigrant labour ("sending money home"); establishment of enterprises abroad, and the movement of the surplus value obtained; profits of steamship companies, etc. We shall still return to this. At present we only wish to note that "world economy" includes all these economic phenomena which, all in all, are based on the relations between human beings en-

[1] Karl Marx, *l.c.*, p. 44.

gaged in the process of production. By and large, the whole process of world economic life in modern times reduces itself to the production of surplus value and its distribution among the various groups and sub-groups of the bourgeoisie on the basis of an ever widening reproduction of the relations between two classes—the class of the world proletariat on the one hand and the world bourgeoisie on the other.

World economy is one of the species of social economy in general. By social economy the science of political economy understands, first of all, a system of individual economies inter-linked by exchange. From this point of view it is perfectly obvious that "social economy" by no means presupposes an "economic subject" guiding the totality of economic relations. What political economy has in mind here, is not economy as a planned "teleological entity" conducting "economic activities," but, first of all, an unorganised system of economies devoid of a conscious collective management where, on the contrary, the economic laws are the elemental laws of the market and of production subordinated to the market. This is why the term social economy in general, as well as the term world economy in particular, by no means requires "regulation" as an indis-pensable defining characteristic.

"Up to the present time the national economic organisms have proved unable to exercise a general regulating influence on the international market where anarchy continues to pre-vail, since this is the battle-ground of the national inter-ests" (*i.e.*, the interests of the "national" commanding classes. —*N.B.*[1]). Notwithstanding this fact, world economy remains world economy.[2]

[1] Paul Stähler: *Der Giroverkehr, seine Entwickelung und internationale Ausgestaltung*, Leipzig, 1909, p. 127.
[2] These remarks are directed against the faulty understanding of the term "world economy" which is widespread in literature. Thus Kalwer proposes the term "economy of the world market" ("Weltmarktwirtschaft"). According to Harms, only international treaties make the term "world economy" ap-plicable to the modern epoch. According to Kobatsch (*vide* his *La politique économique internationale*, Paris, 1913), world economy necessarily presup-poses a world state. We may note in passing that when we speak of world economy we presuppose classification according to the scope of economic connections, not according to the difference in methods of production. This is why it is absurd to blame the Marxists (as Harms does) for allegedly seeing a Socialist economy behind the capitalist economy, while not seeing world economy. Harms simply confuses classifications belonging to entirely different levels.

CHAPTER II

Growth of World Economy

1. Extensive and intensive growth of world economy.
2. Growth of productive forces of world economy. Technique. 3. Production of coal, iron ore, cast iron, copper, gold. 4. Production of other goods. 5. Transport industry: railroads, ocean transport. Telegraph and ocean cables. 6. Growth of foreign trade. 7. Migration. 8. Movement of capital (capital export) and its forms. 9. Participation in, and financing of, foreign enterprises (activities of industrial enterprises and banks).

The growth of international economic connections, and consequently the growth of the system of production relations on a world-wide scale, may be of two kinds. International connections may grow in scope, spreading over territories not yet drawn into the vortex of capitalist life. In that case we speak of the extensive growth of world economy. On the other hand, they may assume greater depth, become more frequent, forming, as it were, a thicker net-work. In that case we have an intensive growth of world economy. In actual history, the growth of world economy proceeds simultaneously in both directions, the extensive growth being accomplished for the most part through the annexationist policy of the great powers.[1]

The extraordinarily rapid growth of world economy, particularly in the last decades, is due to the unusual development of the productive forces of world capitalism. This is directly expressed in technical progress. The most important technical acquisition of the last decade is the production of electrical energy in various forms, and its transmission over distances.

[1] "In the manufacturing period, the division of labour within society was greatly accelerated by the expansion of the world market, and by the colonial system, both of which form part of the general conditions of existence of the period in question." (Karl Marx: *Capital*, Vol. I, p. 373.) This is true also in relation to our present time.

The transmission of electrical energy over a distance rendered production, to some extent, independent of the place where the energy is generated; the latter may be utilised where, not long ago, this was absolutely impossible. This applies, first of all, to the utilisation of water power for the production of electrical energy, "white coal" appearing now side by side with "black coal" as the major factor in the technical production process. Water turbines have come into existence, furnishing energy in previously unheard of quantities. The technique of electricity has exercised an unusually great influence also on the development of steam turbines. Electric light, application of an electro-technical process in the metallurgic industry, etc., must be noted. Internal combustion motors have also acquired a tremendous influence over economic life. The gas motor received a great impetus for development when it became possible economically to utilise the gases of the blast furnaces. Fluid substances here also play the rôle of sources of energy, primarily kerosene and benzine; the Diesel motor has become of general use, manifesting a tendency to replace the old steam engine as antiquated.[1] The use of over-heated steam, numerous discoveries in the application of chemistry, particularly in the dyeing business, a complete revolution in transportation facilities (transportation by electricity, automobiles), wireless telegraph, telephone, etc., complete the general picture of a feverishly rapid technical progress. Never has the union of science with industry achieved greater victories. The rationalisation of the productive process has assumed the form of very close co-operation between abstract knowledge and practical activity. Special laboratories are established in large plants; a special profession of "inventors" (*vide* Edison) is being developed; hundreds of scientific societies for the advancement of special fields of investigation and research are being formed.

The number of patents applied for may serve as a certain indication of technical progress. The number of patents granted progressed in the following way:

[1] Konrad Matschoss: *Grundriss der technisch-geschichtlichen Entwickelung,* (in *Die Technik im XX. Jahrhundert,* herausgegeben von A. Miethe), I. Band.

PATENTS GRANTED

UNITED STATES		GERMANY		ENGLAND		FRANCE	
Years	No. of Patents	Years	No. of Patents	Years	No. of Patents	Years	No. of Patents
1840—	473	1900—	8,784	1860-69—	21,910	1850—	1,687
1860—	4,778	1905—	9,600	1880-87—	30,360	1880—	6,057
1880—	13,917	1910—	12,100	1900—	13,170	1900—	10,997
1900—	26,499	1911—	12,640	1905—	14,786	1905—	11,463
1907—	36,620[1]	1912—	13,080[2]	1908—	16,284[3]	1907—	12,680[4]

Together with technical progress the quantity of extracted and manufactured products increases. The figures relating to the so-called heavy industry are in this respect most indicative, since, with the growth of social productive forces, they are continually being regrouped in a way as to give preponderance to the production of constant capital and particularly of its basic part. The development of the productivity of social labour proceeds in such a way that an ever greater part of that labour is applied to preparatory operations for the production of the means of production; the production of means of consumption, on the contrary, is limited to a relatively diminishing portion of society's labour as whole, and this is the reason why the quantity of the means of consumptions as use-values grows *in natura* in monstrous proportions. Economically, this process expresses itself, among other things, in an ever higher organic composition of social capital, in a continuous growth of the constant capital as compared with the variable capital, and in a lowering of the rate of profit. But while capital, divided into a constant and a variable part, continually increases its constant part, the latter reveals an unequal growth of its component value elements. If we divide the constant capital into fixed and circulating capital (to the latter, as a general rule, the variable capital belongs), there will be revealed a tendency to an ever greater increase of

[1] Augustus D. Webb: *New Dictionary of Statistics*, p. 450.
[2] Webb, *l. c.*, p. 450; *Statistisches Jahrbuch für das Deutsche Reich.*
[3] Webb, *l. c.*, p. 449.
[4] *Ibid*, p. 450.

HEAVY INDUSTRY—WORLD PRODUCTION

COAL		IRON ORE		CAST IRON		COPPER		GOLD	
Years	Millions of metric tons	Years	Thousands of metric tons	Years	Thousands of metric tons	Years	Thousands of metric tons	Years	Millions of pounds sterling
1850	82.6	1850	11,500.0	1850	4,750	1850	52.0	1850	12
1875	283.0	1860	18,000.0	1875	14,119	1880	156.5	1880	22
1880	344.2	1880	43,741.0	1900	41,086	1900	561.0	1900	52
1890	514.8	1890	59,560.1	1901	41,154	1901	586.0	1905	78
1900	771.1	1900	92,201.2	1902	44,685	1902	557.0	1906	83
1901	793.2	1901	88,052.7	1903	47,057	1903	629.0	1907	85
1902	806.7	1902	97,134.1	1904	46,039	1904	654.0	1908	91
1903	883.1	1903	102,016.9	1905	54,804	1905	751.0	1909	93
1904	889.9	1904	96,267.8	1906	59,642	1906	774.0	1910	94
1905	940.4	1905	117,096.3	1907	61,139	1910	891.0	1911	95
1906	1,003.9	1906	129,096.3	1911	64,898	1911	893.8	1912	96
1907	1,095.9[1]	1910	139,536.8[3]	....	......	1912	1,018.6	1913	93
1911	1,165.5[2]	....	......	....	......	1913	1,005.9[4]	1914	91[5]

[1] Juraschek: "Bergbaustatistik," in Handwörterbuch der Staatswissenschaften.
[2] Statistische Jahrbücher des Deutschen Reiches, 1913; the figures are below the real production, as for Asia, Africa, and Australia, the 1910 figures were used.
[3] Juraschek, l.c. The last year is computed according to Statistische Jahrbücher, etc.
[4] Juraschek: "Eisen und Eisenindustrie," in Statistische Jahrbücher.
[5] Statesman's Year-Book, 1915; Juraschek, l.c.; Webb, l.c.

fixed capital. In its essence, this is an expression of the law according to which (taking the growth of the productivity of labour as a prerequisite) the preliminary production operations (the production of means of production) absorb an ever greater part of social energy.[1]

This explains the gigantic growth of the mining and metallurgic industries. If the degree of a country's industrialisation serves as a general indication of its economic progress (*Industriestaat* vs. *Agrarstaat*), then the specific weight of a country's heavy industry may serve as an indication of the economic growth of an industrialised country. This is why the rise of the economic forces of world capitalism finds its most striking expression in the growth of the heavy industries.

Thus in a period of a little over sixty years (beginning from 1850) the production of coal has increased more than 14 times (1,320 per cent), the production of iron ore, more than 12 times (1,113 per cent), that of cast iron, over 13 times (1,266 per cent), that of copper, more than 19 times (1,834 per cent), that of gold, over 13 times (1,218 per cent).[2]

If we now turn our attention to other products, mainly consumption goods produced for the market (*Welthandelsartikel*), we find the increase in their production expressed in the figures in the table on p. 33.

In a period of about thirty years (1881-1889 to 1914) the production of wheat has increased 1.6 times (67 per cent), that of cotton (1884-1890 to 1914-1915) 2.2 times (127 per cent), that of sugar (cane and beet sugar combined) for the period 1880 to 1914-1915, more than 3.5 times (261 per cent), etc.

These figures are more eloquent than words could be. Huge masses of products are being thrown out of the production

[1] Marx was the first to discover this law, and gave a splendid analysis of its function in his examination of the causes of the falling rate of profit (*Capital*, Vol. III, Part I). Modern bourgeois political economy which, in the person of Böhm-Bawerk, declares Marx's entire theory to be a house of cards, plagiarises all the more diligently certain portions of his theory, covering up the traces that lead to the source, such as Böhm-Bawerk's theory of the "by-ways of production" (*Produktionsumwege*), which is a poor version of Marx's law of the growing organic composition of capital.

[2] *Vestnik Finansov*, No. 6, 1915. Gold serves here as a medium of circulation. The table shows that its production grows considerably despite the tremendous rôle of credit and the economy in circulation media in general.

FOODSTUFFS, COTTON, AND RUBBER—WORLD PRODUCTION

WHEAT		COTTON		SUGAR		COCOA		COFFEE		RUBBER	
Years	Millions of tons	Years	Thousands of bales	Years	Thousands of tons	Years	Thousands of tons	Years	Thousands of tons	Years	Thousands of tons
1881–89	...	1884–90	8,591	1880	3,670	....	...	1875	513	......	...
1900	67	1890–96	10,992	1895	7,830	1895–99	82	1892	710	1900	50
1905–07	90	1896–1902	13,521.6	1904–05	11,797	1900–04	119	1903	1,168	1901–02	57
1908	87	1902–08	16,049.6	1907–08	14,125	1907	149.9	1905–06	1,000	1902–04	57
1909	96.9	1911–12	20,529.9	1911–12	13,270	1908	193.6	1906–07	1,500	1906–07	72[4]
1910	99.1	1912–13	19,197.9	1912–13	15,404	1909	205.2	1908	1,100	...	...
1912	105.6	1913–14	20,914.6	1913–14	16,081	1910	216[3]	...	...	...	...
1913	109.5	1914–15	19,543.5[1]	1914–15	13,252[2]	...	...	...	...	...	...
1914	100.1	......		...	...	...	...	...	...	...	...

[1] *Vestnik Finansov*, Nos. 19 and 30, 1915, (concerning cotton). Figures for wheat quoted from Friedrich and *Vestnik Finansov*, No. 15.

[2] Webb, *l.c.*; *Statesman's Year-Book*, 1915.

[3] Friedrich, *l.c.*

[4] *Ibid.*

process to enter into the channels of circulation. The old markets could not have absorbed a hundredth part of what is now absorbed by the world market every year. The world market presupposes not only a certain level of development of production in the strict sense of the word; one of its material conditions of existence is the development of the transportation industry. The more developed the transport facilities, the faster and the more intensive the movement of commodities, the faster is the process of welding together the individual, local and "national" markets, the faster is the growth of the world economy's production organism as a unit. Such is in modern economic life the rôle of steam and electric transportation. The railroad mileage by the middle of the last century (1850) was 38,600 kilometers; by 1880 the figure grew to 372,000 kilometers.[1] Since then the length of the railroad tracks has grown with astounding rapidity.

LENGTH OF RAILROAD TRACKS IN KILOMETERS

	End of 1890	End of 1911
Europe	223,869	338,880
United States of America	331,417	541,028
Asia	33,724	105,011
Australia	18,889	32,401
Total	607,899	1,017,320[2]

During twenty years (1890-1911), the length of the railroad tracks increased 1.71 times (171 per cent).

The same development may be observed in the merchant marine. Marine transportation, be it noted, plays an exclusive rôle, since it alone facilitates the movement of commodities from continent to continent ("transoceanic trade"), but its rôle is also greatly due to its comparative cheapness even as far as Europe is concerned. Compare the movement of commodities between the Black and the Baltic Seas. The following figures illustrate the growth of marine transportation:

[1] Professor Wiedenfeld: "Eisenbahnstatistik," in *Handwörterbuch der Staatswissenschaften.*
[2] *Statistisches Jahrbuch für das Deutsche Reich,* 1913.

MARINE TRANSPORTATION
Increase in Percentages

Countries	1872 to 1907	1890 to 1907
English Merchant Marine	184	106
German Merchant Marine	281	166
French Merchant Marine	70	96
Norwegian Merchant Marine ...	64	7
Japanese (1885–1907)	1,077	52 [1]

World ship-building for commercial purposes has grown in the last years as follows:

WORLD SHIP-BUILDING

Years	Tons
1905	2,514,922
1906	2,919,763
1907	2,778,088
1908	1,833,286
1909	1,602,057
1910	1,957,853
1911	2,650,140
1912	2,901,769
1913	3,332,882
1914	2,852,753 [2]

According to Harms,[3] the tonnage of the world merchant marine grew 55.6 per cent between 1899 and 1909 alone. This gigantic growth of marine transportation has made it possible to unite the economic organisms of several continents and to revolutionise the pre-capitalist methods of production in the most backward corners of the world, thus accelerating world commodity circulation in astounding proportions. The latter, however, is accelerated not in this way alone. In reality the entire movement of the capitalist mechanism is much more complicated, since commodity circulation and the rotation of capital do not necessarily presuppose that commodities are changing their places in space.

[1] G. Lecarpentier: *Commerce maritime et marine marchande*, Paris, 1910, p. 53.
[2] *Statesman's Year-Book*, 1915.
[3] Harms, *l. c.*, p. 126.

Within the rotation of capital and metamorphoses of commodities which are a part of that rotation, the mutation process of social labour takes place. These mutation processes may require a change of location on the part of the products, their transportation from one place to another. Still a circulation of commodities may take place without their change from place to place, and a transportation of products without the circulation of commodities or even without a direct exchange of products. A house which is sold by A to B does not wander from one place to another, although it circulates as a commodity. Movable commodity values, such as cotton or iron, remain in the same warehouse at a time when they are passing through dozens of circulation processes when they are bought and sold by speculators. That which really changes its place here is the title of ownership, not the thing itself.[1]

Similar processes take place also in modern times in gigantic proportions due to the development of the most abstract form of capitalism, to the ever growing impersonal character of capital, to the growth of the volume of stocks and bonds as an expression of the form of property that is characteristic for our times, in a word, due to the growth of "stock" capitalism (Liefmann) or "finance" capitalism (Hilferding). The international leveling of commodity prices and of stock and bond values is accomplished by wire (activities of the stock and commodity exchanges). The network of telegraphs grows with the same feverish tempo as the means of transportation. Of particular importance is the increase in the length of cables connecting various continents. By the end of 1913, there were 2,547 cables (the number has already increased to 2,583); the length of all these cables was 515,578 kilometers.[2] The length of the cables is equal to half the length of all the railroads of the world (which in 1911 was 1,057,809 kilometers). Thus there grows an extremely flexible economic structure of world capitalism, all parts of which are mutually inter-dependent. The slightest change in one part is immediately reflected in all.

We have so far examined the technical and economic prerequisites of world economy. Let us now examine the process

---

[1] Karl Marx: *Capital,* Vol. II, translated by Ernest Untermann, p. 169.
[2] *Statistisches Jahrbuch für das Deutsche Reich,* 1913, p. 39; *The Statesman's Yearbook.*

itself. We have seen that the most primitive form in which economic interdependence expresses itself in a system of commodity economy, is exchange. The category of world prices expresses this interdependence on a world scale. An outward expression of the same phenomonon is the international movement of commodities, "international trade." Although the figures quoted below cannot pretend to be absolutely accurate, they correctly reflect the persistent trend towards widening the sphere of the world market.

FOREIGN TRADE (BOTH EXPORT AND IMPORT) OF THE
LEADING COUNTRIES OF THE WORLD

Years	Millions of Marks
1903	101,944.0
1904	104,951.9
1905	113,100.6
1906	124,699.6
1907	133,943.5
1908	124,345.4
1909	132,515.0
1910	146,800.3
1911	153,870.0 [1]

INCREASE IN FOREIGN TRADE BETWEEN 1891 AND 1910

Countries	Import (per cent)	Export (per cent)
United States	78	77
England	43	52
Germany	105	107
France	25	54
Russia	100	85
Holland	110	90
Belgium	105	84
British India	75	62
Australia	35	74
China	64	79
Japan	300	233 [2]

Thus, within eight years, from 1903 to 1911, international trade increased 50 per cent—a very substantial increase indeed.

[1] Ibid.
[2] Harms, l.c., p. 212.

38   IMPERIALISM AND WORLD ECONOMY

The quicker the pulse of economic life, the faster the growth of the productive forces, the wider and deeper goes the process of internationalisation of economy. W. Sombart's thesis of the diminishing importance of international relations (*abnehmende Bedeutung der weltwirtschaftlichen Beziehungen*) is therefore absolutely incorrect.[1] This most paradoxical of modern economists had paid a certain tribute long before the war, to the imperialistic ideology which, he said, strives towards economic "autarchy" and creates a large self-sufficient whole.[2] His "theory" is a generalisation of the fact that the home sale of *manufactured goods* in Germany grew faster than the export of such goods. It is from this fact that Sombart drew a queer conclusion concerning the diminishing significance of foreign trade in general. However, as Harms [3] correctly remarks, even assuming that manufactured goods gravitate towards the internal market more than towards foreign markets (a conclusion to which Sombart arrives from the analysis of German data only), one must not, on the other hand, overlook the increasing import of raw materials and foodstuffs which serve as a prerequisite for the home trade in manufactured goods, for the internal market, since it is due to such an import that the country is not compelled to waste productive forces on the production of raw materials and food. Definite conclusions can be drawn only after an analysis is made of both sides of the international exchange and of the distribution of productive forces in all the branches of social production. The tendencies of modern development are highly conducive to the growth of

[1] W. Sombart: *Die deutsche Volkswirtschaft im XIX. Jahrhundert;* Berlin, 1913.
[2] Sombart, who during the war turned into a raving imperialist, is not an isolated phenomenon. In analysing the economic problems connected with world economy, one may discern two trends. One is optimistic, the other demands first of all a strengthening of the inner forces of an imperialist nation fighting for power, hence this trend pays great attention to the problems of the internal market. See, for instance, Dr. Heinrich Pudor, "Weltwirtschaft und Inlandproduktion," in *Zeitschrift für die gesamte Staatswissenschaften,* herausgegeben von K. Bücher, 71. Jahrgang (1915) 1. Heft, which says that "we must strive towards German world economy (*deutsche Weltwirtschaft*), insofar only as our production, our industry, seizes ever greater markets and unsaddles foreign competition. In that case, [he says] world trade expands accordingly. The foundation, however, must be home (*heimische*) production" (pp. 147-148).
[3] Harms, *l.c.,* p. 202, footnote; also Sigmund Schilder: *Entwickelungstendenzen der Weltwirtschaft,* Berlin, 1912-15.

international relations of exchange (and with them many others), in that the industrialisation of the agrarian and semi-agrarian countries proceeds at an unbelievably quick tempo, a demand for foreign agricultural products is created in those countries, and the dumping policy of the cartels is given unusual impetus. The growth of world market connections proceeds apace, tying up various sections of world economy into one strong knot, bringing ever closer to each other hitherto "nationally" and economically secluded regions, creating an ever larger basis for world production in its new, higher, non-capitalist form.

If the international movement of commodities expresses the "mutation process" in the socio-economic world organism, then the international movement of the populations expresses mainly the redistribution of the main factor of economic life, the labour power. Just as within the framework of "national economy" the distribution of labour power among the various production branches is regulated by the scales of wages which tend to one level, so in the framework of world economy the process of equalising the various wage scales is taking place with the aid of migration. The gigantic reservoir of the capitalist New World absorbs the "superfluous population" of Europe and Asia, from the pauperised peasants who are being driven out of agriculture, to the "reserve army" of the unemployed in the cities. Thus there is being created on a world scale a correspondence between the supply and demand of "hands" in proportions necessary for capital. An idea of the quantitative side of the process may be gleaned from the following figures:

NUMBER OF IMMIGRANTS ENTERING U. S. A.

Years	
1904	812,870
1905	1,026,499
1906	1,100,735
1907	1,285,349
1914	1,218,480[1]

[1] D. Lewin: *Der Arbeitslohn und die soziale Entwickelung*, Berlin, 1913, p. 141; also U. Philippov: *Emigration*, p. 13. The last figure is taken from the *American Year-Book* for 1914, p. 385.

NUMBER OF FOREIGNERS IN GERMANY

Years

1880	276,057
1900	778,737
1910	1,259,873 [1]

In 1912, 711,446 emigrated from Italy, 467,762 from England and Ireland, 175,567 from Spain (1911), 127,747 from Russia, etc.[2] To this number of final emigrants, *i.e.*, of workers who relinquish their fatherland forever and look for a new country, must be added a number of emigrants of a temporary and seasonal character. Thus the Italian emigrants are mostly of a temporary character; Russian and Polish workers immigrate into Germany for agricultural work (the so-called *Sachsengängerei*, etc.). These ebbs and flows of labour power already form one of the phenomena of the world labour market.

Corresponding to the movement of labour power as one of the poles of capitalist relations is the movement of capital as another pole. As in the former case the movement is regulated by the law of equalisation of the wage scale, so in the latter case there takes place an international equalisation of the rates of profit. The movement of capital, which from the point of view of the capital exporting country is usually called capital export, has acquired an unrivalled importance in modern economic life, so that some economists (like Sartorius von Waltershausen) define modern capitalism as export capitalism (*Exportkapitalismus*). We shall touch upon this phenomenon in another connection. At present we only wish to point out the main forms and the approximate size of the international movement of capital which forms one of the most essential elements in the process of internationalising economic life, and in the process of growth of world capitalism. Export capital is divided into two main categories. It appears either as capital yielding interest, or as capital yielding profits.

Inside of this division one can discern various sub-species

---

[1] Lewin, *l.c.*, p. 141.
[2] *Statistisches Jahrbuch für das Deutsche Reich*, etc.

and forms. In the first place, there are state and communal loans. The vast growth of the state budgets, caused both by the growing complexity of economic life in general, and by the militarisation of the entire "national economy," makes it ever more necessary to contract foreign loans to defray the current expenses. The growth of large cities, on the other hand, demands a series of works (electric railways, electric light, sewage system and water supply, pavements, central steam heat, telegraph and telephone, slaughter houses, etc., etc.), which require large sums of money for their construction. These sums are also often obtained in the forms of foreign loans. Another form of capital export is the system of "participation," where an enterprise (industrial, commercial, or banking) of country A holds stocks or bonds of an enterprise in country B. A third form is the financing of foreign enterprises, creating of capital for a definite and specified aim; for instance, a bank finances foreign enterprises created by other institutions or by itself; an industrial enterprise finances its branch enterprise which it allows to take the form of an independent corporation; a financing society finances foreign enterprises.[1] A fourth form is credit without any specified aim (the latter calls for "financing") extended by the large banks of one country to the banks of another country. The fifth and last form is the buying of foreign stocks, etc., with the purpose of holding them (compare activities of banks of issue), etc. (The last of the enumerated forms differs from the others in that it does not create a lasting community of interests.)

In various ways there thus takes place the transfusion of capital from one "national" sphere into the other; there grows the intertwining of "national capitals"; there proceeds the "internationalisation" of capital. Capital flows into foreign factories and mines, plantations and railroads, steamship lines and banks; it grows in volume; it sends part of the surplus value "home" where it may begin an independent movement; it accumulates the other part; it widens over and over again the sphere of its application; it creates an ever thickening net-

[1] For more about such companies see R. Liefmann: *Beteiligungs-und Finanzierungsgesellschaften*, Jena, 1913.

work of international interdependence.   The numerical side of
the process may be partly realised from the following:

FRENCH CAPITAL IN 1902

CAPITAL INVESTED ABROAD		NATURE OF INVESTMENTS	
Countries	*Billions of Francs*	*Enterprises*	*Millions of Francs*
Russia	9–10.0	Trade	995.25
England	0.5	Real Estate	2,183.25
Belgium and Holland	0.5	Banks and Insur-	
Germany	0.5	ance Business...	551.00
Turkey, Serbia and		Railroads	4,544.00
Bulgaria	0.5	Mining and Indus-	
Roumania and Greece	3–4.0	try	3,631.00
Austria-Hungary	2.0	Marine Transport,	
Italy	1–1.5	Harbors, etc. ...	461.00
Switzerland	0.5	State and Commis-	
Spain and Portugal ..	3.5	sion Loans	16,553.50
Canada and U.S.A...	0.5	Miscellaneous	936.00
Egypt and Suez	3–4.0		
Argentina, Brazil and		Total	29,855.00 [2]
Mexico	2.3–3.0		
China and Japan	1.0		
Tunis and French			
Colonies	2–3.0		
Total	30–35.5 [1]		

Leroy-Bolieu computes for 1902 the figure of French capital
invested in foreign enterprise and loans as equal to 34 billion
francs.[3]   In 1905 the figure had already reached 40 billion
francs.   The total value of stocks and bonds in the Paris stock
exchange was, for 1904, 63,990 million francs in French securities plus 66,180 million francs in foreign securities; for
the year 1913 the respective figures were 64,104 and 70,761.[4]

[1] Harms, *l.c.*, pp. 228-229.
[2] Sartorius von Waltershausen: *Das volkswirtshaftliche System der Kapi-
talanlage im Auslande*, Berlin, 1907, p. 56.
[3] *Economiste Français*, 1902, II, p. 449 (quoted by Sartorius).
[4] Sartorius von Waltershausen, *l.c.*; *Vestnik Finansov*, 1915, No. 4.

ENGLAND

ENGLISH CAPITAL INVESTED ABROAD (1911)		FOREIGN SECURITIES PLACED IN ENGLAND (State Railways, Mining Loans and Loans of Various Corporations)	
Countries	Pounds Sterling	Year	Million Pounds Sterling
English Colonies and India	1,554,152,000	1892	49.9
U. S. A.	688,078,000	1893	29.9
Cuba	22,700,000	1894	52.2
Philippines	8,202,000	1895	55.2
Mexico	87,334,000	1896	56.1
Brazil	94,330,000	1897	47.4
Chile	46,375,000	1898	59.8
Uruguay	35,255,000	1899	48.2
Peru	31,896,000	1900	24.2
Other American Countries	22,517,000	1901	32.6
Russia	38,388,000	1902	57.7
Turkey	18,320,000	1903	54.3
Egypt	43,753,000	1904	65.3
Spain	18,808,000	1905	102.6
Italy	11,513,000	1906	61.0
Portugal	8,134,000	1907	68.9
France	7,071,000	1908	121.9
Germany	6,061,000	1909	121.9
Other European Countries	36,317,000	1910	132.7 [1]
Japan	53,705,000		
China	26,809,000		
Other Foreign Countries	61,907,000		
Total (excluding English Colonies)	1,637,684,000		
Total (including English Colonies)	3,191,836,000		

[1] Harms, l. c., p. 235.

English capital invested in foreign countries, including English colonies, amounted at the beginning of 1915, according to Lloyd George's statement, to four billion pounds sterling.

As to Germany, figures relative to the placing of foreign securities and to the quotation of foreign securities on the German stock exchange show a decline of the latter (according to the *Statistisches Jahrbuch für das Deutsche Reich* for 1913, the nominal value of admitted securities was in 1910, 2,242 million marks, in 1911, 1,208 million marks, in 1912, 835 million marks), but this seeming decline in capital export is explained by the fact that the German banks are buying securities in increasing quantities at the foreign exchanges, especially in London, Paris, Antwerp, and Brussels, and also by the "financial mobilisation of capital" for the purposes of war. The total of German investments abroad amounts to some 35 billion marks.

GERMANY

Countries	Millions of Marks	Countries	Millions of Marks
Argentina	92.1	Luxembourg	32.0
Belgium	2.4	Mexico	1,039.0
Bosnia	85.0	Holland	81.9
Brazil	77.6	Norway	60.3
Bulgaria	114.3	Austria	4,021.6
Chile	75.8	Portugal	700.7
Denmark	595.4	Roumania	948.9
China	356.6	Russia	3,453.9
Finland	46.1	Serbia	152.0
Great Britain	7.6	Sweden	355.3
Italy	141.9	Switzerland	437.6
Japan	1,290.4	Spain	11.2
Canada	152.9	Turkey	978.1
Cuba	147.0	Hungary	1,506.3

A word or two about Belgian capital whose investment abroad amounts to 2.75 billion francs. Its total is distributed among the various countries as follows:

BELGIUM

Countries	Millions of Francs
U. S. A.	4,945.8
Holland	70
France	137
Brazil	143
Italy	166
Egypt	219
Germany	244
Argentina	290
Congo	322
Spain	337
Russia	441
Others	338 [1]

The United States, while importing large amounts of capital, exports considerable quantities of it into Central and South America, especially into Mexico, Cuba, and Canada.

The finance system of Cuba was the first to attract the attention of the capitalists of the United States. Americans own large plantations in Cuba. American enterprise helped considerably in developing the neighbouring Mexican republic, particularly in building and utilising the Mexican railroads. It was natural that the Mexican 5 and 4 per cent loans (amounting to $150,000,000.00) should have been placed on the market of the United States. The 4 per cent loan of the Philippine Islands was also placed on the American market. In Canada the United States placed over $590,000,000.00, in Mexico over $700,000,000.00, etc.[2]

Even such countries as Italy, Japan, Chile, and others play an active part in this great migration of capital. The general direction for the movement is, of course, indicated by the difference in the rates of profit (or the rate of interest): the more developed the country, the lower is the rate of profit, the greater is the "over-production" of capital, and consequently the lower is the demand for capital and the stronger the ex-

[1] Harms, l. c., p. 242; Schilder: *Entwickelungstendenzen der Weltwirtschaft*, p. 364 ff.
[2] M. Bogolepov: "The American Market," in *Vestnik Finansov*, 1915, No. 39.

pulsion process. Conversely, the higher the rate of profit, the lower the organic composition of capital, the greater is the demand for it and the stronger is the attraction.

In the same way as the international movement of commodities brings the local and "national" prices to the one and only level of world prices; in the same way as migration tends to bring the nationally different wage scales for hired workers to one level, so the movement of capital tends to bring the "national" rates of profit to one level, which tendency expresses nothing but one of the most general laws of the capitalist mode of production on a world scale.

We must dwell here with greater detail on that form of capital export which expresses itself in "participating in" and "financing" of foreign enterprises. Within the framework of world economy the concentration tendencies of capitalist development assume the same organisational forms as are manifest within the framework of "national" economy: namely, there come more strikingly to the foreground the tendencies towards limiting free competition by means of forming monopoly enterprises. It is in this process of forming monopoly organisations that participation and financing play a very large part. If we were to follow up "participation" in its various stages, to be judged by the number of acquired shares, we would realise how complete fusion is gradually being prepared. When you own a small number of shares, you can take part in shareholders' meetings; when you own a greater number of shares, you establish a closer contact with the enterprise (you can try to share with the enterprise new production methods or patents, you can speak of dividing the market, etc.), a certain community of interests is thus established; if you own more than 50 per cent of the shares, your "participation" already amounts to complete fusion. Quite wide-spread is the practice of establishing branches in the form of nominally independent corporations whose funds, however, are held by their "mother" corporation (*Muttergesellschaft*).[1] The latter phenomenon is often observed in international relations. To avoid legal obstacles in a "foreign" country and to be able to

[1] R. Liefmann: *Beteiligungs- und Finanzierungsgesellschaften*, pp. 47-48. It must be noted that under certain conditions "control" and fusion can be achieved with much less than 50 per cent of the shares.

use the privileges of native industrialists in the new "father-land," branches are being established in those countries under the guise of independent corporations.

Thus the cellulose factory of Waldhof in Mannheim has (or we may now use the past tense) a Russian branch in Pernov; the bronze paint factory, Carl Schlenk, Inc., in Nuremburg, has an American "daughter corporation"; the same is true of Varziner Papierfabrik, which has an American branch known as the Hammerville Paper Company; the largest cable enter-prise on the continent, the Westfälische Drahtindustrie, has a daughter corporation in Riga, etc. Conversely, foreign cor-porations have branches in Germany and other countries; for instance, the Maggi corporation of Kempttal, Switzerland, has branches in Singen and Berlin, Germany, also in Paris (Com-pagnie Maggie and Société des boissons hygiéniques). In 1903 the American Westinghouse Electric Company, Pittsburgh, or-ganised a branch near Manchester, England; in 1902 the Amer-ican Diamond Match Company, having gradually increased its participation in an enterprise located in Liverpool, finally ab-sorbed it, and reduced it to the state of a branch of the American main firm, etc.[1] The same is true of numerous Swiss chocolate factories and weaving enterprises, English soap fac-tories, machine shops and twine factories, American sewing machine factories, machine plants, etc.

One must not think, however, that participation in foreign enterprises is limited to this form alone. In reality there are a great many forms of "participation" of various degrees, from ownership of a comparatively insignificant number of shares, particularly when a given enterprise (commercial, industrial, or banking) "participates" simultaneously in several enter-prises, to ownership of nearly all the shares. The mechanism of "participation" consists in the fact that a given corporation issues its own stocks and bonds with the purpose of acquiring the securities of other enterprises. Liefmann distinguishes three forms of such "substitution of securities" (*Effektensub-stitution*) which he classifies according to the aim of the respective "substituting corporations" (*Substitutionsgesell-schaften*): 1) "Investment Trust" where the "substitution of

[1] Sartorius von Walterhausen, *l.c.*, p. 174.

securities" is made with the purpose of receiving dividends from more lucrative, if more risky, enterprises; 2) "Placement Societies" (*Effektenübernahmegesellschaften*) whose aim it is to place the securities of enterprises whose stocks and bonds, in consequence of legal or material difficulties, cannot be placed in the hands of the public directly; 3) "Holding Companies" (*Kontrollgesellschaften*) which buy up the securities of various enterprises, eliminating them from circulation and replacing them by securities of the holding company, which thus acquires influence over these enterprises without spending its own capital. The aim is clearly influence, "control," *i. e.*, practical domination over given enterprises.

In all these cases it is assumed that the securities to be replaced are already in existence. Where the latter have to be created, we have before us the financing operation which, as we have seen, may be carried out by banks, industrial and commercial enterprises, also special "financing companies." In so far as the financing is done by industrial enterprises, it is ordinarily connected with the establishment of foreign branches, since it is there that the new securities are being issued.

The financing enterprises may have a very wide range of activities. Thus the mechanical enterprise Orenstein Koppel—Arthur Koppel, Inc., has founded ten "daughter companies," of which the largest are located in Russia, Paris, Madrid, Vienna, and Johannesburg (South Africa); the firm of Körting Bros. in Hanover has branches in Austria, Manchuria, France, Russia, Belgium, Italy, Argentina; numerous German cement plants have "daughter companies" in the United States; German chemical plants have branches in Russia, France, and England; the Norwegian nitrate enterprises are to a very large extent financed by foreign capital. The Norwegian, French, and Canadian capitalists have formed the Norsk Hydro Elektrisk Kvälstofaktieselskab (also known as Société Norvégienne de l'Azote et des Forces Hydro-Electriques), which in its turn has founded two companies with participation also of German capital. The greatest internationalisation of production has been attained in the electrical industry. The Siemens Halske firm has its enterprises in Norway, Sweden, South Africa, and Italy; it has branches in Russia, England, and Austria. The famous Allgemeine Elektrizitätsgesellschaft (for short, A-E-G) has its daughter companies in London, Petrograd, Paris, Genoa, Stockholm, Brussels, Vienna, Milan, Madrid, Berlin, in American cities, etc; similar activities are shown by the Thomson-Houston Company and by its successor, the General Electric Company, by the Singer Manufacturing Company, the Dunlop Pneumatic Tire Company, etc.[1]

The large banks naturally play a very large part in financing foreign enterprises. A glance at the activities of those institutions shows how strong the international connections of "national" organisations have already grown. A 1913 report of the Société Générale de Belgique declares its "national" securities to be equal to 108,322,425 francs, whereas its foreign securities were equal to 77,899,237. The latter capital is invested in enterprises and loans of such diverse countries as Argentina, Austria, Canada, China, Congo, Egypt, Spain, the United States, France, Morocco, New Caledonia, Russia, etc.[2] Data concerning the activities of the German banks have been worked out in great detail. We quote here facts relating to the largest German banks as typical of the entire banking business of Germany.

Die Deutsche Bank. 1) Founded the Deutsche Ueberseeische Bank with 23 branches: 7 in Argentina, 4 in Peru, 2 in Bolivia, 1 in Uruguay, 2 in Spain, 1 in Rio de Janeiro; 2) founded, together with the Dresdner Bank, the Anatolische Eisenbahngesellschaft (Société du chemin de fer Ottoman D'Anatolie); 3) bought, together with the Wiener Bankverein, the shares of the Betriebsgesellschaft der orientalischen Eisenbahnen; 4) founded the Deutsche Treuhandgesellschaft operating in America; 5) participates in the Deutsch-Asiatische Bank, Shanghai; 6) participates in the Bank für orientalische Eisenbahnen, Zürich; 7) participates in the Banca Commerciale Italiana, Milan; 8) participates in the Deutsch-Atlantische,

---

[1] Liefman, *l.c.*, pp. 99-104. Of course, financing may be extended not only to branches of the same firm. Thus the firm of Knop, together with the Soloviev Brothers and the Kraft Brothers, financed in 1912 the Caspian Manufacture, a partnership organisation that had acquired the property of a liquidated association formed in the province of Daghestan by the Moscow financier Reshetnikov, the Siberian banker Petrokokino and by the Paris-Netherland Bank (*Birzhevye Vyedemosti*, April 15, 1915).

[2] *La Vie Internationale*, Vol. V, 1914, p. 449 (Published by the *Office Centrale des Associations Internationales*. Brussels).

Ost-Europäische, Deutsch-Niederländische Telegraphengesellschaft, the Norddeutsche Seekabelwerke and the Deutsch-
Südamerikanische Telegraphengesellschaft; 9) participates in
the Schantung-Bergbau and in the Schantung-Eisenbahngesell-
schaft; 10) participates, together with Turkish, Austrian, German, French, Swiss and Italian firms, in the Imperial Ottoman
Society of the Bagdad Railroad; 11) founded the Ost-Afrikanische Gesellschaft; 12) participates in the Deutsch-Ost-Afrikanische Bank; 13) participates, together with Swiss and German firms, in the Zentral-Amerika-Bank (later known as Aktiengesellschaft für überseeische Bauunternehmungen); 14)
participates in the banking firm of Güterbook, Horwitz & Co.,
Vienna; 15) participates in the firm of Ad. Goerz, Berlin (the
firm operates mines in Johannesburg).

Diskonto-Gesellschaft. 1) Participates in the Deutsche
Handels- und Plantagengesellschaft der Südseeinseln and in the
Neu-Guinea-Kompagnie; 2) founded, together with the Nord-
Deutsche Bank, the Brasilianische Bank für Deutschland with
five branch banks; 3) participates, together with other banks,
in the Deutsch-Asiatische Bank; 4) participates in the banking firm of Ernesto Tornquist, Buenos-Aires, and in the firm
of Albert de Bary & Co., Antwerp, that is connected with the
former; 5) participates in the Banca Commerciale Italiana;
6) founded, together with the Nord-Deutsche Bank, the Bank
für Chile und Deutschland, with eight branches; 7) founded,
together with the firm of Bleichröder, the Banca Generale
Romana in Bucharest (now has six branches); 8) participates,
together with many firms, in the Banque Internationale de
Bruxelles; 9) participates in the Schantung-Eisenbahngesell-
schaft, the Schantung-Bergbaugesellschaft, and in a number
of cable and telegraph enterprises; 10) founded the Otavi-
Minen- und Eisenbahngesellschaft, Africa; 11) founded the
Ost-Afrikanische Eisenbahngesellschaft; 12) participates in
the Deutsch-Ost-Afrikanische Bank; 13) founded, together
with Bleichröder, a Bulgarian firm and the Nord-Deutsche
Bank, the Kreditna Banka in Sophia; 14) founded, together
with Woermann, Hamburg, the Deutsch-Afrika-Bank; 15)
participates in the General Mining and Finance Corporation
Ltd., London; 16) founded, together with other firms, the

Kamerun-Eisenbahngesellschaft; 17) opened a branch bank in London in 1900; 18) financed, together with Krupp, the Grosse Venezuela-Eisenbahn; 19) participated, as a member of the Rothschild banking trust, in Austro-Hungarian, Finnish, Russian, and Roumanian state railways, loans, industrial enterprises, etc.[1]

Similar activities are shown by the other large banks of Germany, the Dresdner Bank, the Darmstädter Bank, Berliner Handelsgesellschaft, Schaffhausen'scher Bankverein, and Nationalbank für Deutschland, which also have a number of daughter societies in common throughout the countries of the world.[2]

Of course, it is not the German banks alone that develop such intensive activities abroad. A comparison of figures would show that England and France are in the lead. While the foreign banks of German origin numbered only 13 by the beginning of 1906 (with 100 million marks of capital, and 70 branch banks), England possessed by the end of 1910 36 colonial banks with branches in London, and with 3,358 local bureaus in the colonies, also 36 other banks in foreign countries with 2,091 branches. France, in 1904-5, possessed 18 colonial and foreign banks with 104 branches; Holland, 16 foreign banks with 68 branches, etc. Individual banks of France also show great economic power in relation to the colonies and foreign countries. Thus, in 1911, the Crédit Lyonnais had about 16 branches abroad, and 5 in Algeria; the Comptoir National d'Escompt had 12 branches abroad, and 11 in Tunis and Madagascar; the Société Générale and the Crédit Industriel have branches only in London, but on the other hand they have numerous daughter companies abroad.[3]

"Participation," and "financing" as a further step in participation, signify that industry is being moulded to an ever

[1] Dr. Jacob Riesser: *Die deutschen Grossbanken und ihre Konzentration im Zusammenhang mit der Entwickelung der Gesamtwirtschaft in Deutschland,* fourth edition, 1912, p. 354. [English translation: J. Riesser: *The German Great Banks and their Concentration in Connection with the Economic Development of Germany,* Washington, Government Printing Office, 1911. Further references to this volume are to the German edition.—*Trans.*]

[2] Riesser, *l.c.*, p. 371 *ff.*

[3] *Ibid.*, p. 375. The rapid *growth* of the German banks deserves attention. There were only 4 of them by the end of the nineties, 6 in 1903, with 32 branch banks, and 13 in 1906, with 70 branch banks.

growing degree into one organised system. The most modern types of capitalist monopoly in their most centralised forms, like the trusts, are only one of the forms of "participating companies" or "financing companies." They enjoy a more or less monopolistic ownership of the capitalist property of our times, and they are looked upon and classified, from the point of view of the movement of securities, as a specific expression of the capitalist property of our times.

We thus see that the growth of the world economic process, having as its basis the growth of productive forces, not only calls forth an intensification of production relations among various countries, not only widens and deepens general capitalist interrelations, but also calls to life new economic formations, new economic forms unknown to the past epochs in the history of capitalist development.

The beginnings of the organisation process that characterises the development of industry within "national" economic boundaries, become ever more evident also against the background of world economy relations. Just as the growth of productive forces within "national" economy, on a capitalist basis, brought about the formation of national cartels and trusts, so the growth of productive forces within world capitalism makes the formation of international agreements between the various national capitalist groups, from the most elemental forms to the centralised form of an international trust, ever more urgent. These formations will be the object of our inquiry in the next chapter.

CHAPTER III

Organisation Forms of World Economy

1. ANARCHIC STRUCTURE OF WORLD ECONOMY. 2. INTERNATIONAL SYNDICATES AND CARTELS. 3. INTERNATIONAL TRUSTS. 4. INTERNATIONAL BANK SYNDICATES. 5. NATURE OF INTERNATIONAL, PURELY CAPITALIST ORGANISATIONS. 6. INTERNATIONALISATION OF ECONOMIC LIFE AND INTERNATIONALISATION OF CAPITALIST INTERESTS.

WORLD economy in our times is characterised by its highly anarchic structure. In this respect the structure of modern world economy may be compared with the structure of "national" economies typical till the beginning of this century, when the organisation process, briskly coming to the fore in the last years of the nineteenth century, brought about substantial changes by considerably narrowing the hitherto unhampered "free play of economic forces." This anarchic structure of world capitalism is expressed in two facts: world industrial crises on the one hand, wars on the other.

It is a profound error to think, as the bourgeois economists do, that the elimination of free competition and its replacement by capitalist monopolies would do away with industrial crises. Such economists forget one "trifle," namely, that the economic activities of a "national" economy are now conducted with a view towards world economy. As to the latter, it is by no means an arithmetical total of "national" economies, just as a "national" economy is by no means an arithmetical total of individual economies within the boundaries of the state territory. In either case, there is a very substantial element supplementing all the others, namely, connections, reciprocal action, a specific medium which Rodbertus called "economic communication," without which there is no "real entity," no "system," no social economy, only isolated economic units. This is why, even if free competition were entirely eliminated within the boundaries of "national economies," crises would

53

still continue, as there would remain the anarchically established connections between the "national" bodies, *i. e.*, there would still remain the anarchic structure of world economy.[1]

What was said about crises is true also about wars. War in capitalist society is only one of the methods of capitalist competition, when the latter extends to the sphere of world economy. This is why war is an immanent law of a society producing goods under the pressure of the blind laws of a spontaneously developing world market, but it cannot be the law of a society that consciously regulates the process of production and distribution.

Still, notwithstanding the fact that modern world economy as a whole represents an anarchic structure, the process of organisation is making strides even here, expressing itself mainly in the growth of international syndicates, cartels, and trusts. We shall, first of all, undertake a general survey of these formations of modern times.

In the transport industry the largest cartels are (barring the changes brought about by the war): 1) the Sailing Shipowners Documentary Committee (English, German, Norwegian and Danish maritime societies); 2) the Internationale Segelschiffahrtkonvention (English, German, Danish, Swedish and Norwegian sail boats); 3) the Baltic and White Sea Conference embracing from 60 to 70 per cent of the total Baltic and White Sea tonnage (combining Germans, Frenchmen, Dutchmen, Englishmen, Spaniards, Belgians, Danes, Norwegians, Swedes, Russians, and Finns); 4) the Internationaler Küstenschiffahrtsverband, Altona; 5) the Nordatlantischer Dampferlinienverband (Germans, Americans, Belgians, Frenchmen, and Austrians); 6) the International Mercantile Marine Company, alias The Morgan Trust (mainly Americans, Englishmen, and Germans) which, by the end of 1911, owned 130 steamships with a gross tonnage of 1,158,270 tons. Outside of these car-

---

[1] This is beginning to dawn even upon bourgeois writers. Thus Mr. Goldstein says: "That the cartels and trusts are in no position to eliminate crises, is seen, among other things, from the fact that the steel trust, in whose hands, including affiliated enterprises, something like 90 per cent of the U. S. production of steel were concentrated, utilised by the end of the first quarter of 1908 only one-half of the production capacity of its plants, etc." (I. M. Goldstein: *Syndicates, Trusts, and Modern Economic Policies*, second edition, Moscow, 1912, p. 5, footnote). *Cf.* also Tugan Baranovsky: *Industrial Crises.*

tels of a higher type, there exists a number of important agreements as to the regulation of freight rates, rebates, etc.

In the mining and metallurgic industries: 1) the Internationales Trägerkartell (steel syndicates of Germany, Belgium and France); 2) the Internationales Schienenkartell (German, English, French, Belgian, American, Spanish, Italian, Austrian, and Russian rail works); 3) the Internationale Stahlkonvention (the American Steel Trust, the Bethlehem Steel Company, and the Krupp firm); 4) the Internationale Bleikonvention (German, Australian, Belgian, American, Mexican and English lead manufacturers); 5) the Deutsch-Oesterreichischer Stahlgussverband; 6) the Deutsch-Englische Ferromanganeisenkonvention; 7) the Internationale Vereinigung von Ferrasiliziumwerke (Norwegians, Swiss, Tyrolians, Bosnians, Savoyians, and Germans); 8) the Internationales Metallplattensyndikat (Germans and Austrians); 9) the Vereinigung der Zinkplattenfabrikanten (Englishmen and Americans; very influential in the world market); 10) the Internationale Zinkkonvention (Germans, Belgians, Frenchmen, Italians, Spaniards, Englishmen, and Americans; controls 92 per cent of the European output); 11) Internationaler Zinkhüttenverband (Germans, Frenchmen, Belgians, Englishmen); 12) Internationales Drahtgeflechtekartell (Germans, Belgians, Frenchmen, Englishmen); 13) Internationales Abkommen der Kupferdrahtziehereien; 14) Deutsch-Englische Schraubenkonvention; 15) Internationales Emaillekartell (Germans, Austro-Hungarians, Frenchmen, Swiss, Italians); 16) Internationales Turbinensyndikat (mainly Germans and Swiss); 17) Vereinigte Dampfturbinengesellschaft (German A-E-G, American General Electric Co. and other firms); 18) Automobiltrust (Motor Trade Association and nearly all the outstanding European automobile enterprises); 19) Russisch-Deutsch-Oesterreichisches Syndikat für landwirtschaftliche Geräte; 20) Internationale Vereinigung von Eisenwarenhändlerverbänden (Germans, Englishmen, Frenchmen, Austro-Hungarians, Swiss, Belgians); 21) Internationaler Verband der Korsettschliessen und Federnfabriken (nearly all large factories in existence).

The stone, clay, etc., industry has six large international cartels.

In the electrical industry, as we have noted above, the process of the internationalisation of production finds its most salient expression. There are several very large international agreements in existence. The largest are: 1) an agreement between the German A-E-G, the American General Electric Company, and the British-French Thomson Houston Company, the organisation having a network of enterprises spread over every part of the world; 2) Internationales Galvanosteginsyndikat; 3) Verkaufstelle Vereinigter Glühlampenfabriken (Germans, Austro-Hungarians, Swedes, Dutch, Italians, Swiss); there are, besides, numerous special agreements between banks concerning the financing of electric enterprises etc.

In the chemical industry, international cartelisation has become pronounced, mainly in a number of particular fields. The more important are: 1) Internationales Chlorkalk-kartell (Germans, Frenchmen, Belgians, Englishmen, Americans); 2) Internationales Leimkartell (glue factories in Austria-Hungary, Germany, Holland, Belgium, Sweden, Denmark, and Italy, sales office in London); 3) Internationales Boraxkartell (Germans, Americans, Frenchmen, Austro-Hungarians, Englishmen); 4) Internationaler Verband der Seidenfärbereien (German, Swiss, French, Italian, Austrian and American associations of dyers); 5) Internationales Karbidsyndikat (all European); 6) Internationales Pulverkartell; 7) Deutsch-Oesterreichischer Superfosphatkartell; 8) Kartell der Belgisch-Holländischen Oleinproduzenten; 9) Internationale Verkaufsvereinigung Stickstoffdünger (German, Norwegian, Italian, and Swiss factories of nitrate fertiliser); 10) Internationales Kerosinkartell (Standard Oil Company and Russian firms); 11) Verband Deutsch-Oesterreichisch-Italienischer Kipsgerber und Kipshändler; 12) Internationales Salpetersyndikat; 13) Internationales Koalinverkaufsyndikat (Austro-Germans); 14) Europäische Petroleumunion (Germans, Englishmen, Swiss, Dutch, Belgians, Austrians, Danes, Americans, East-Asiatic oil producers).

In the textile industry the international agreements concern themselves mainly with special branches of production: 1) the International Federation of Master Cotton Spinners and Manufacturers Association (representing the continental-European and American industry); 2) Deutsch-Oesterreichisches Kravatenstoffkartell; 3) Internationales Samtindustriekartell (all the German and French velvet factories); 4) Kunstseide Verkaufskontor (German and Belgian factories of artificial silk); 5) International Cotton Mills Corporation (U. S. A. and the rest of America); 6) Konvention der deutschen und schweizerischen Seidencachenezfabrikanten; 7) Verband der deutschschweizerischen Cachenez- und Kravattenfabrikanten; 8) Oesterreichisch-Deutsches Jutekartell; 9) Internationaler Verband der Kratzenfabriken (Germans, Luxemburgians, Belgians, Dutch, Austro-Hungarians, Swedes, Norwegians, Danes, Balkanites); 10) Internationale Nähseidekonvention (Austrian, Belgian, Russian, Spanish and English enterprises); 11) Internationale Vereinigung der Flachs- und Werggarnspinner (nearly all the large flax spinners of Europe); 12) Internationales Kartell der Schappenspinner.

In the glass and china industry, the largest international organisation is the Europäischer Verband der Flaschenfabrikanten (embracing nearly all the European countries); also a number of large glass and china cartels.

The paper industry numbers seven large international cartels.

Ten other agreements concerning six different industries (rubber, cabinetmaking, cork, cocoa, etc.) are also known to exist.[1]

Besides the above mentioned cartels, there exist hundreds of international trusts (mergers and controlling organisations). We shall mention here only the most outstanding, i.e., such as have the greatest economic weight in the world market.

Such a trust is the Standard Oil Company of New Jersey which, in 1910, owned the shares of 62 companies (including the Anglo-American Oil Company, the Deutsch-Amerikanische Petroleumgesellschaft, and the Romana-Americana) and was connected with a very large number of enterprises and companies (Dutch, German, French, Swedish, Italian, Russian, Swiss, etc.).[2] The trust "controls" the Amalgamated Copper

---

[1] The list of international cartels is here reproduced from the above quoted book by Harms (p. 254 ff.). We quote this list as well as the list of international trusts and bank syndicates because, as far as we know, there is no Russian literature dealing with the question.

[2] Liefmann, l.c., p. 249 ff.

Company which is intent on acquiring a world monopoly in the production of copper. Another large trust is the United States Steel Corporation, the largest "controlling company" in the world. Of the other trusts, the outstanding are: Reisemühlen und Handelsaktiengesellschaft in Barmen, with foreign participation equalling 6,039,344 marks;[1] the Internationale Bohrgesellschaft; the Nobel Trust Company; a number of international trusts in the petroleum industry; the banana trust organised by the Boston Fruit Company and the Tropical Trading and Transport Company; the packing trust; the sewing thread trust with the English firm of J. and P. Coats, Ltd., at its head; the Société Centrale de la Dynamite; Compagnie Générale de la Conduits d'Eau (Lüttich) which "controls" enterprises in Utrecht, Barcelona, Paris, Naples, Charleroi, Vienna; the Trust metallurgique belge-français, etc., etc.[2]

Behind all these cartels and trusts, as a rule, stand the enterprises that finance them, *i.e.*, primarily the banks. The internationalisation process whose most primitive form is the exchange of commodities and whose highest organisational stage is the international trust, has also called into being a very considerable internationalisation of banking capital in so far as the latter is transformed into industrial capital (by financing industrial enterprises), and in so far as it thus forms a special category: finance capital.

It is finance capital that appears to be the all-pervading form of capital, that form which, like nature, suffers from a *horror vacui*, since it rushes to fill every "vacuum," whether in a "tropical," "sub-tropical," or "polar" region, if only profits flow in sufficient quantities. We quote below a number of examples of gigantic international banking trusts to illustrate the friendly "mutual aid" given by the large "national" banks to one another.

In 1911, a finance trust, the Société financière des valeurs américaines, was organised at Brussels with the aim of financing American enterprises. It included the Deutsche Bank and the firm of Warburg Company in Hamburg, the Société Générale

---

[1] *Ibid.*, p. 275.
[2] Kobatsch, *l.c.*; Liefmann, *l.c.*; Harms, *l.c.*

in Brussels, the Banque de Bruxelles, the Banque de Paris et de Pays-Bas, the Société Générale pour favoriser l'industrie nationale in Paris, the Société Français de banques et de dépôts, the Banque Française pour le Commerce et l'Industrie, Kuhn-Loeb Company, New York, etc., etc.—all of them belonging to the largest banks of the world.[1] The Deutsche Bank that forms part of that "finance trust," organises, together with the Schweizerische Kreditanstalt and the Speyer-Ellissen firm, the Aktiengesellschaft für überseeische Bauunternehmungen for the purpose of organising building enterprises on the other side of the ocean; it organises centres for the sale of kerosene in several countries; it forms an alliance with the Russian firm of Nobel; it participates in the European Kerosene Union.[2] Not so long ago, a banking trust (Consortium Constantinopel) was organised in Brussels for the purpose of financing enterprises in Constantinople. It includes the Deutsche Bank, the Deutsche Orientbank (connected with the former), the Dresdner Bank, the Schaffhausenscher Bankverein, the Nationalbank, the Société Générale in Paris, the Banque de Paris, the Comptoir National, the Schweizerische Kreditanstalt, and the Bank für elektrische Unternehmungen.[3] A special railroad bank is organised in Belgium (the Banque belge de chemins de fer) with the aid of the Banque de Paris et de Pays-Bas, the Wiener Bankverein, the Schweizerische Kreditanstalt, the Société Générale des chemins de fer économiques, the Deutsche Bank, the Dresdner Bank, etc., i.e., with the aid of an international banking trust. One more example: the Russian Metal Syndicate was aided by four groups of "national" banks—the Russian group (Asov Commerce Bank, St. Petersburg International Commerce Bank, Russian Foreign Commerce Bank, Russo-Asiatic Bank, and Commerce Bank in Warsaw); the French group (Crédit Lyonnais, Banque de Paris et de Pays-Bas, Société Générale); the German group (Deutsche Bank, Bank für Handel und Industrie, and Dresdner Bank); and the Belgian group

---

[1] Liefmann, *l.c.*, p. 174.
[2] Liefmann, *l.c.*, pp. 456-486.
[3] *Ibid.*, pp. 497-498.

(Crédit Général à Liège, Société Générale de Belgique, Nagel-märkers fils à Liège).[1]

It would be a great error to think that all these examples are accidental exceptions. Economic life is teeming with them. Colonial enterprises, and the export of capital to other continents, railway construction and state loans, city railways and ammunition firms, gold mines and rubber plantations, all are intrinsically connected with the activities of international banking trusts. International economic relations are extended through countless threads; they pass through thousands of cross-points; they are intertwined in thousands of groups, finally converging in the agreements of the largest world banks which have stretched out their tentacles over the entire globe. World finance capitalism and the internationally organised domination of the banks are one of the undeniable facts of economic reality.

On the other hand, one must not overestimate the significance of international organisations. Their specific weight compared with the immensity of the economic life of world capitalism is by no means as great as would appear at the first glance. Many of them (*i.e.*, of the syndicates and cartels) are only agreements concerning the division of markets (*Rayonierungs-kartelle*); in a series of large subdivisions of social economy they embrace only very specific branches of production (such as the bottle syndicate which is one of the strongest); many of them are of a highly unstable nature. Only those international agreements which are based on a natural monopoly are possessed of a greater degree of stability. Still, there is a tendency towards a continuous growth of international formations, and this growth cannot be ignored when analysing the development of modern world economy.[2]

---

[1] Zagorsky: *Syndicates and Trusts*, p. 230. We mention only private international economic agreements. It is assumed that state agreements, playing an immense economic part (like the International Postal Alliance, the railroad agreements, etc.), are known to the reader.

[2] Sartorius von Waltershausen puts a very low estimate on the part played by international organisations. Compare *l.c.*, p. 100: "That there should be created, and there should exist, international companies with centralised [*einheitlicher*] management of production appears unlikely. But, of course, one may expect that there would be agreements between large national companies concerning the distribution of the selling markets." The opposite point of view is maintained by Harms.

We have pursued the main tendencies in the growth of world economy from the exchange of commodities up to the activities of international banking syndicates. This process in all its ramified forms is the process of the internationalisation of economic life; the process of bringing separate geographic points of economic development closer to each other; the process of reducing capitalist relations to one level; the process of the growing contrast on the one hand between concentrated property in the hands of the world capitalist class, and on the other, the world proletariat. It does not follow from this, however, that social progress has already reached a stage where "national" states can co-exist harmoniously. For the process of the internationalisation of economic life is by no means identical with the process of the internationalisation of capital interests. A Hungarian economist was perfectly right when he remarked concerning the works of the English pacifist, Norman Angell, that "he" (*i.e.*, Norman Angell) "forgets only one thing: that there are classes both in Germany and England, and that the thing that may be superfluous, useless, even harmful, for the people as a whole, can be of very great benefit (*sehr gewinnbringend sein kann*) for individual groups (large financiers, cartels, bureaucracy, etc.)." [1] This proposition can, of course, be applied to all states, for their class structure is beyond any doubt, at least from a purely scientific point of view. This is why only those who do not see the contradictions in capitalist development, who good-naturedly assume the internationalisation of economic life to be an *Internationale der Tatsachen, i.e.*, those who assume anarchic internationalisation to be organised internationalisation—can hope for the possibility of reconciling the "national" capitalist groups in the "higher unity" of peaceful capitalism. In reality things take place in a much more complicated way than appears to the opportunist optimists. The process of the internationalisation of economic life can and does sharpen, to a high degree, the conflict of interests among the various "national" groups of the bourgeoisie. Indeed, the growth of international commodity exchange is by

[1] Erwin Szabo: "Krieg und Wirtschaftsverfassung," in *Archiv für Sozialwissenschaft und Sozialpolitik*, 39. Bd., 3. Heft, pp. 647-648.

no means connected with the growth of "solidarity" between the exchanging groups. On the contrary, it can be accompanied by the growth of the most desperate competition, by a life and death struggle. The same is true of the export of capital. "Community of interests" is not always created in this field. Competitive struggle for the spheres of capital investment may here, too, reach a highly acute state. There is only one case in which we can say with assurance that solidarity of interests is created. This is the case of growing "participation" and financing, *i.e.*, when, due to the common ownership of securities, the class of capitalists of various countries possesses collective property in one and the same object. Here we actually have before us the formation of a golden international;[1] there is apparent here, not a simple similarity or, as one is wont to say at present, a "parallelism" of interests; there is actual unity here; but the course of economic development creates, parallel to this process, a reverse tendency towards the nationalisation of capitalist interests. And human society as a whole, placed under the iron heel of world capital, pays tribute to this contradiction—in unbelievable torment, blood, and filth.

The perspectives of development can be pointed out only after analysing all the main tendencies of capitalism. And since the internationalisation of capitalist interests expresses only one side of the internationalisation of economic life, it is necessary to review also its other side, namely, that process of the nationalisation of capitalist interests which most strikingly expresses the anarchy of capitalist competition within the boundaries of world economy, a process that leads to the greatest convulsions and catastrophes, to the greatest waste of human energy, and most forcefully raises the problem of establishing new forms of social life.

We are thus confronted with the task of analysing the process of the nationalisation of capital.

---

[1] How the ideologists of the present-day bourgeoisie view this golden international (we do not speak, of course, of the contradistinction between the "top" and the "bottom") may be seen from the following statement by Sartorius: "The 'golden international' can never be an ideal for a man who has a fatherland, and who believes that in that fatherland are sunk the roots of his existence" (*l.c.*, p. 14). This in turn shows the *comparative weakness* of the process of the internationalisation of capitalist interests.

PART II

WORLD ECONOMY AND THE PROCESS OF
NATIONALISATION OF CAPITAL

CHAPTER IV

The Inner Structure of "National Economies" and the Tariff Policy

1. "NATIONAL ECONOMIES" AS INTERSECTIONS OF WORLD ECONOMIC RELATIONS. 2. GROWTH OF MONOPOLY ORGANISATIONS. CARTELS AND TRUSTS. 3. VERTICAL CONCENTRATION. COMBINED ENTERPRISES. 4. ROLE OF THE BANKS. TRANSFORMATION OF CAPITAL INTO FINANCE CAPITAL. 5. BANKS AND VERTICAL CONCENTRATION. 6. STATE AND COMMUNAL ENTERPRISES. 7. THE SYSTEM AS A WHOLE. 8. THE TARIFF POLICY OF FINANCE CAPITAL, AND CAPITALIST EXPANSION.

WORLD economy, as we have seen above, represents a complex network of economic connections of the most diverse nature; the basis of this are production relations on a world scale. Economic connections uniting a great number of individual economies are found to become more numerous and more frequent as we proceed, within the framework of world economy, to analyse "national" economies, *i.e.*, economic connections existing within the boundaries of individual states. There is nothing mysterious about this; we must not attribute that fact to an alleged creative rôle of the "state principle" that is supposed to create from within itself special forms of national economic existence; neither is there a predestined harmony between society and state. The matter has a much simpler explanation. The fact is that the very foundation of modern states as definite political entities was caused by economic needs and requirements. The state grew on the economic foundation; it was only an expression of economic connections; state ties appeared only as an expression of economic ties. Like all living forms, "national economy" was, and is, engaged in a continuous process of internal regeneration; molecular movements going on parallel with the growth of productive forces, were continually changing the position of individual "national" economic bodies in their relation to each other, *i.e.*, they influenced the interrelations of the individual parts of the growing world economy. Our time produces highly significant relations. The destruction, from top to bottom, of old, conservative, economic forms that was begun with the initial stages of capitalism, has triumphed all along the line. At the same time, however, this "organic" elimination of weak competitors inside the framework of "national economies" (the ruin of artisanship, the disappearance of intermediary forms, the growth of large-scale production, etc.) is now being superseded by the "critical" period of a sharpening struggle among stupendous opponents on the world market. The causes of this phenomenon must be sought first of all in the internal changes that have taken place in the structure of "national capitalisms," causing a revolution in their mutual relations.

Those changes appear, first of all, as the formation and the unusually rapid spread of capitalist monopoly organisations: cartels, syndicates, trusts, bank syndicates.[1] We have seen above how strong this process is in the international sphere. It is immeasurably greater within the framework of "national economies." As we shall see below, the "national" carteling of industry serves as one of the most potent factors making for the national interdependence of capital.

[1] We cannot dwell here at length on the differences between those economic forms. For our purposes here, suffice it to be said that we do not see any fundamental difference between cartels and trusts, the trust in our opinion being only a more centralised form of the same phenomenon. All purely formal attempts (compare, for instance, Eduard Heilmann, "Ueber Individualismus and Solidarismus in der kapitalistischen Konzentration" in Jaffe's *Archiv*, Bd. 39, Heft 3) at defining the difference between the two forms by saying that the trust is "autocratic" while the syndicate (or cartel) is "democratic," does not in the least tackle the real issue, the latter being the outcome of the part played by those formations in the national economic life. It does not follow, however, that there is no difference at all between them; on the contrary, from a certain point of view, one must emphasise the difference. At any rate, the difference does not lie on the level of the distinction between the "democratic" and "autocratic" principle. See corresponding chapters in Hilferding's *Finanzkapital*. Briefly, the difference is that "contrary to the process of trustification, cartelisation by no means signifies the elimination of a conflict of interests between the individual enterprises belonging to the cartel" (Hilferding: "Organisationsmacht und Staatsgewalt," *Neue Zeit*, 32. Jahrgang, 2. Bd., p. 140 ff.).

The process of the formation of capitalist monopolies is, logically and historically, a continuation of the process of concentration and centralisation of capital. Just as the free competition of artisans, arising over the bones of feudal monopoly, led to the accumulation of the means of productions in the hands of the class of capitalists as their monopoly possession, so free competition inside of the class of capitalists is being more and more limited by restrictions and by the formation of giant economies monopolising the entire "national" market. Such giant economies must by no means be considered "abnormal" or "artificial" phenomena springing up in consequence of state aid like tariffs, freight rates, premiums, subsidies, or governmental orders, etc. True, all these "causes" have materially accelerated the process of monopolisation, but they have never been, and are not, its prime condition. What is really a *conditio sine qua non* is a certain degree of concentration of production. This is why, generally speaking, monopoly organisations are the strongest where productive forces are most developed. A particularly important part was played in this respect by joint stock companies, a form that has immensely facilitated the investment of capital in production and has created enterprises of hitherto unknown dimensions. It is therefore most natural that leadership in the cartel movement belongs to the two countries that have forged ahead with feverish rapidity to the first places in the world market, namely, the United States and Germany.

The United States represents a classic example of modern economic development, and it is here that the most centralised form of monopoly organisations, the "trusts," have become deeply rooted. The following table gives a clear idea of the tremendous economic power of the trusts—of the largest trusts in particular—as well as of their growth.

According to Moody, the growth of trusts between 1904 and 1908 is expressed in the figures in the table below.

According to *Poor's Manual of Corporations* and *Poor's Manual of Railroads* for 1910, the total equals 33.3 billion dollars.[1] By 1910, the share of the trusts in "national" pro-

---

[1] *Ibid.* Also George Renard and A. A. Dulac: *L'évolution industrielle et agricole depuis cent cinquante ans*, Paris, 1912, p. 204.

Groups of Trusts	1904		1908	
	No. of Companies	Value of Stocks and Bonds	No. of Companies	Value of Stocks and Bonds
Seven Largest Industrial Trusts ..	1,524	2,662,752,100	1,638	2,708,438,754
Smaller Industrial Trusts	3,426	4,055,039,433	5,038	8,243,175,000
Trusts in process of Reorganisation	282	528,551,000	....	....
Total	5,232	7,246,342,533	6,676	10,951,613,754
Concession Enterprises	1,336	3,735,456,071	2,599	7,789,393,600
Group of largest Railroads	1,040	9,397,363,907	745	12,931,154,010
Total	7,608	20,379,162,511	10,020	31,672,161,354 [1]

duction was already very large. They produced 50 per cent of the textiles, 54 per cent of the glassware, 60 per cent of the cotton and printed goods, 62 per cent of the foodstuffs, 72 per cent of the alcoholic beverages, 77 per cent of the metal products (exclusive of iron and steel), 81 per cent of the chemicals, 84 per cent of the iron and steel.[2] Since then their share in the national production has grown considerably, for the process of concentration and centralisation of capital in the United States proceeds with magic rapidity.

Only a few students of the most recent development of the finance organisation of large-scale production and its commercial branches can have an idea of the gigantic concentration, and of its power over combined and differentiated large-scale enterprises, which often include productive forces reaching beyond the boundaries of an individual national economy.[3]

[1] Prof. Nazarevsky: *Outline of the History and Theory of Capitalist Collective Economy, Syndicates, Trusts, and Combined Enterprises,* Vol. I, part I, *Outline of the History of Combinations in American Industry,* Moscow, 1912, pp. 318-319.
[2] L. Goldstein: *Syndicates, Trusts, and Modern Economic Policy,* Moscow, 1912, p. 51.
[3] Eugen von Phillipovich: "Monopole und Monopolpolitik," in Grünberg's *Archiv für die Geschichte des Sozialismus und der Arbeiterbewegung,* Bd. VI (1915), Heft I, p. 158.

Within the framework of the present study it is impossible even to enumerate the chief trusts operating in the various countries. Let it be noted only that at the head of all of them are the two most colossal trusts, the Standard Oil Company and the United States Steel Corporation, respectively representing the two financial groups of Rockefeller and Morgan.

The movement of big capital in Germany proceeds along identical lines. By 1905 there were, according to official statistics, 385 cartels in the most diverse branches of production.[1] The well-known theoretician and leader of the cartel movement in Germany, Dr. Tschierschky, estimates the number of cartels in Germany as between 550 and 600.[2] The greatest among them are: the Rhine-Westphalian Coal Syndicate (*Rheinisch-Westfälisches Kohlensyndikat*) and the Steel Syndicate (*Stahlwerksverband*). According to Raffalovich, the former produced in 1909, in the Dortsmund region, 85 million tons of coal, whereas the production of all the "outsiders" amounted to 4,200,000 tons only (4.9 per cent).[3] By January, 1913, the production of syndicate coal amounted to 92.6 per cent of the total production in the Ruhr region and 54 per cent of the total national production. By that time the steel syndicate had increased its production to 43-44 per cent of the national production. The sugar refining trust, embracing 47 enterprises, produces a very large share of the total output (70 per cent of the sugar consumed in the country, and 80 per cent of the sugar exported abroad).[4] The electric trust (an *Interessengemeinschaft* between two trusts: the Siemens-Schuckert and the A-E-G) control 40 per cent of all the power produced.

The monopoly organisations in other countries are less formidable, but taken in absolute numbers, without comparison with the United States or Germany, the syndication process is considerable everywhere.

France numbers a considerable array of syndicates in the metallurgic, sugar, glass, paper, naphtha, chemical, textile, coal, etc., industries. Of particular importance are Le Comptoir de

[1] Robert Liefmann: *Kartelle und Trusts*, Stuttgart, 1910.
[2] Dr. S. Tschierschky: *Kartell und Trust*, Leipzig, Göschen, 1911, p. 52.
[3] A. Raffalovich: "Les syndicats et les cartels en allemagne en 1910," in *Revue internationale de commerce, de l'industrie et de la banque*, July 30, 1911.
[4] Martin Saint Léon: *Cartels et Trusts*, 3me ed., Paris, 1909, p. 56.

Longway which produces almost all the cast iron manufactured in France; the sugar syndicate, which dominates the market almost completely; the Société Générale des glaces de St. Gobain, which also occupies an almost absolute monopoly situation, etc; a series of agricultural syndicates, close to which are the agricultural societies,[1] must also be noted, as well as the large combinations in the transportation industry, namely, the three steamship companies (Compagnie Générale Trans- atlantique, Compagnie des Messageries Maritimes, and Com- pagnie des Chargeurs Réunis), which embrace 41.25 per cent of the entire merchant marine of France.[2]

In England, where, despite the great concentration of in- industry, the monopoly movement for a long while remained very weak due to a number of reasons, the trustification of industry ("amalgamations," "associations," and "investment trusts") has made tremendous strides in the very last few years. Old peculiarities begin to recede, to become a thing of the past, both as regards the labour movement in England and as regards the traditional English free trade policy (as we shall see below, free competition, which is only another name for free trade, is being relegated more and more to the back- ground in the realm of economic foreign policy). Only igno- rance can at present refer to England as a representative of an entirely different economic type. Here are a few cases that may serve as an example: the Association of Portland Cement Manufacturers, producing 89 per cent of the national output; the steel trusts; the alcohol trusts; the wallpaper trusts pro- ducing 98 per cent of all the wallpaper and other decorative materials; the cable trusts (the Cablemakers' Association, pro- ducing about 90 per cent of the national output); the salt trust (Salt Union, about 90 per cent); the Fine Cotton Spinners' and Doublers' Trust (practically controlling the entire produc- tion of England); the dyers' and bleachers' trust (Bleachers' Association and Dyers' Association, about 90 per cent); the Imperial Tobacco Company (about one-half of the national production), etc.[3]

[1] Martin Saint Léon, *l.c.*, p. 89 *ff.*
[2] G. Lecarpentier: *Commerce maritime et marine marchande*, Paris, 1910, p. 165.
[3] Hermann Levy: *Monopoly and Competition*, London, 1911, pp. 222-267.

In Austria we find among the large cartels: the coal syndicate of Bohemia (with 90 per cent of all the production of Austria); the brick syndicate with a yearly output amounting to 400 million crowns (the production of outsiders amounting only to 40 million crowns); the iron syndicate; the naphtha syndicate (in Galicia, with 40 per cent of the national output); the sugar, glass, paper, textiles, and other syndicates.

Even in such a backward country as Russia, with such a paucity of capital, the number of higher type syndicates and trusts, according to Mr. Goldstein, exceeds 100. There are, besides, a number of local agreements of a less developed type. Let us note the largest.[1] In the coal industry the Produgol Trust (producing 60 per cent of the coal dug in the Don area); 19 syndicates in the iron industry, among which the most prominent are Prodameta (iron implements trusts, controlling 88-93 per cent of national production), the Krovlia (sheet iron trust, with 60 per cent of the national output), and Prodvagon (railroad car trust, embracing 14 out of the 16 car construction plants); in the oil industry almost the entire production is concentrated in the hands of four companies, mutually interlocked; noteworthy are also the copper syndicate (90 per cent), the sugar syndicate (100 per cent), the textile manufacturers' agreements, the tobacco trust (57-58 per cent), the match syndicate, etc.

The syndicates show a high degree of development in Belgium; but even such young countries as Japan have also entered the road of building capitalist monopolies. The old production forms of capitalism have thus undergone a radical change. According to F. Laur's figures *out of 500 billion francs invested in the industrial enterprises of all the countries of the world, 225 billions, i.e., almost one-half, are invested in production organised in cartels and trusts.* (This capital is distributed in the various countries as follows: United States, 100 billion francs; Germany, 50 billion francs; France, 30 billion francs; Austria-Hungary, 25 billion francs, etc.—all these figures being estimated below the actual ones).[2] This indicates a complete transformation of the old interrelation of

[1] We quote from L. Kafenhaus: *Syndicates in the Russian Iron Industry;* Goldstein, *l.c.;* Zagorsky, *l.c.*
[2] *Goldstein, l.c.,* p. 5.

forces inside every country, which could not fail to entail radical changes in the interrelation of the countries themselves.

The process, however, is not limited to individual branches of production. There is going on a continuous process of binding together the various branches of production, a process of transforming them into one single organisation. This expresses itself, first of all, in the form of combined enterprises, *i.e.*, enterprises combining the production of raw materials and manufactured goods, the production of manufactured goods with that of unfinished products, etc., which process can and does absorb the most diverse branches of production, since under the prevailing division of labour in our times every branch depends upon the other to a larger or lesser degree, directly or indirectly. For instance, when a trust produces outside of its main product also a by-product, it shows a tendency to monopolise this latter branch of production, which in turn serves as a stimulus to monopolising the production of goods used as substitutes for the by-product; then comes the tendency to monopolise the production of raw materials used for the production of the substitute, and so on and so forth. Thus combinations are created which, at first glance, seem astounding, like iron and cement, oil and glucose, etc.[1] This vertical concentration and centralisation of production, in contradistinction to the horizontal centralisation which is going on within one branch of production, signifies, on the one hand, a diminution of the social division of labour, since it combines in one enterprise the labour that was previously divided among several enterprises; on the other hand, it stimulates the division of labour inside of the new production unit. The entire process, taken on a social scale, tends to turn the entire "national" economy into a single combined enterprise with an organisation connection between all the branches of production. The same process is going on with great rapidity in another way: banking capital penetrates industry, and capital turns into finance capital.

We have seen in the preceding chapters what tremendous significance is attached to participation in and financing of industrial enterprises. The latter is one of the functions of modern banks.

[1] Nazarevsky, *l.c.*, p. 354 *ff*.

An increasingly large section of industrial capital does not belong to the industrialists who apply it. The right to manipulate the capital is obtained by them only through the bank which, in relaiton to them, appears as the owner of that capital. On the other hand, the bank is compelled to place an ever growing part of its capital in industry. In this way the bank becomes to an ever increasing degree an industrial capitalist. Bank capital, *i.e.*, capital in money form, which has *thus been in reality transformed into industrial capital, I call finance capital.*[1]

Thus by means of various forms of credit, by owning stocks and bonds, and by directly promoting enterprises, banking capital appears in the rôle of an organiser of industry. This organisation of the combined production of a whole country is the stronger, the greater; on the one hand, the concentration of industry, on the other, the concentration of banking. The latter has of late assumed colossal proportions. Here are a few examples. In Germany an actual monopoly of banking is in the hands of six banks: the Deutsche Bank, the Diskontogesellschaft, the Darmstädter Bank, the Dresdner Bank, the Berliner Handelsgesellschaft, and the Schaffhausenscher Bankverein; the capital of those banks amounted in 1910 to 1,122.6 million marks.[2] The growth of the power of those banks may be seen from the growth of the number of their institutions inside of Germany (counting the main banks and their branches, deposit banks and currency exchange offices, also their "participation" in the German stock company banks): in 1895, 42; in 1896, 48; in 1900, 80; in 1902, 127; in 1905, 194;· in 1911, 450.[3] Within 16 years the number of those institutions grew eleven times.

In the United States there are only two banks of such importance: The National City Bank (the Rockefeller firm) and the National Bank of Commerce (the Morgan firm). Those two banks hold sway over countless industrial undertakings and banks, intertwined in all sorts of ways. "The size of the bank operations of the Rockefeller and Morgan groups may

[1] Rudolf Hilferding: *Das Finanzkapital*, Vienna, 1910, p. 283.
[2] Werner Sombart: *Die Deutsche Volkswirtschaft in XIX. Jahrhundert*, Berlin, 1913, chapter x. According to recent newspaper reports (the *Vorwärts*, Berlin), the Diskontogesellschaft has already swallowed up the Schaffhausenscher Bankverein.
[3] J. Riesser: *Die Deutschen Grossbanken*, Appendix VIII, p. 745.

be approximately judged by the fact that, in 1908, the first group counted among its clients, and held reserves of, 3,350, and the latter of 2,757, national, state and other banks." No new trust can be founded without the aid of these banks, they being a "monopoly of monopoly making." [1]

Corresponding to this unique economic tie between the various production branches and the banks, is a special form of higher management of both. As a matter of fact, the representatives of the industrialists manage the banks, and vice versa. Jeidels is authority for the statement that, in 1903, the six above mentioned German banks held 751 seats in the supervising councils of the industrial stock companies. [2] Conversely, there were (in December, 1910) 51 representatives of industry in the supervising councils of the banks. [3]

As to America, the following fact is highly characteristic. From a list submitted to the Senate during the debate over the bill for the improvement of the banking business (La Follette's commission in 1908), it was evident that 89 persons held over 2,000 directors' posts in various industrial, transportation, and other companies, all of which companies were directly or indirectly controlled by Morgan and Rockefeller.

Mention must be made here also of the important part played by state and communal enterprises, which enter into the general system of "national economy." Among state enterprises we find, first of all, mining (in Germany, e.g., out of 309 coal mines with an output of 149 million tons, 27 mines with an output of 20.5 million tons belonged to the state in 1909; the total value of state production amounted to 235 million marks; salt mines and others also belong to this category; the gross income from all state enterprises of Germany in 1910 amounted to 349 million marks, while the net income was 25 million marks); [4] next to mining are state railroads (only in England, and only prior to the war, were the railroads exclusively in the hands of private owners); then the post office, the telegraph,

---

[1] Nazarevsky, l.c., p. 362.
[2] Parvus: Der Staat, die Industrie und der Sozialismus, p. 77 (Written when Parvus was still in the "first stage" of his transformations). Riesser, l.c., Beilage IV, p. 651 ff.
[3] Riesser, l.c., p. 501.
[4] K. T. Eheberg: Finanzwissenschaft, 1922, p. 99. [The author quotes here from an early Russian translation.—Trans.]

etc., also forestry. Among communal enterprises of great economical importance are mainly the water system, the gas system, and the electric constructions, with all their ramifications.[1]
The powerful state banks also form part of this system. The
interrelation between those "public" enterprises and the enterprises of a purely private character assumes various forms;
the economic connections, in general, are numerous and vari-
egated, and credit is not the least among them. Very close
relations arise on the basis of the so-called mixed system (*gemischte Unternehmungen*) where a certain enterprise is composed of both "public" and private elements (participation
of large-scale, usually monopolistic, firms)—a phenomenon
not infrequent in the realm of communal economy. The example of the German Empire Bank (*Reichsbank*) is of particular
interest. This bank, whose part in the economic life of Germany is tremendous, appears so closely connected with "private economy" that there is an unsettled dispute going on as
to whether it is a stock company or a state institution, whether
it is subject to the laws governing private or public undertakings.[2]

All parts of this considerably organised system, cartels,
banks, state enterprises, are in the process of growing together; the process is becoming ever faster with the growth
of capitalist concentration; the formation of cartels and combines creates forthwith a community of interest among the
financing banks; on the other hand, banks are interested in
checking competition between enterprises financed by them;
similarly, every understanding between the banks helps to tie
together the industrial groups; state enterprises also become
ever more dependent upon large-scale financial-industrial formations, and vice versa. Thus various spheres of the concentration and organisation process stimulate each other, creating a very strong tendency towards transforming the entire
national economy *into one gigantic combined enterprise under*
the tutelage of the financial kings and the capitalist state, an

[1] See *Kommunales Jahrbuch* for 1913-14, published by Lindemann, Schwander
and Südekum, p. 566 *ff.*
[2] See Willy Baumgart: *Unsere Reichbank. Ihre Geschichte und ihre Ver-*
fassung, Berlin, 1915. The rôle of the state as an organiser of industry has
grown tremendously during the war. We shall discuss this later, when dealing
with the future of national and world economy.

enterprise which monopolises the national market and forms the prerequisite for organised production on a higher non-capitalist level.

It follows that world capitalism, the world system of production, assumes in our times the following aspect: a few consolidated, organised economic bodies ("the great civilised powers") on the one hand, and a periphery of undeveloped countries with a semi-agrarian or agrarian system on the other. The organisation process (which, parenthetically speaking, is by no means the aim or the motive power of the capitalist gentlemen, as their ideologists assert, but is the objective result of their seeking to obtain a maximum of profit) tends to overstep the "national" boundaries. But it finds very substantial obstacles on this road. First, it is much easier to overcome competition on a "national" scale than on a world scale (international agreements usually arise on the basis of already existing "national" monopolies); second, the existing differences of economic structure and consequently of production-costs make agreements disadvantageous for the advanced "national" groups; third, the ties of unity with the state and its boundaries are in themselves an ever growing monopoly which guarantees additional profits. Among the factors of the latter category, let us first of all turn our attention to the tariff policy.

The character of the tariff policy has undergone a total transformation. Old-time customs duties aimed at defence; present-day customs duties aim at aggression; old-time tariffs were secured for commodities whose production was so little developed at home that they could not stand competition on the world market; in our days "protection" is accorded to those branches of production which are most capable of withstanding competition.

Friedrich List, that apostle of protectionism, in his *National System of Political Economy,* dealt with *educational* customs duties, looking upon them as upon a temporary measure.

We shall speak here [he says] of tariff legislation only as a means to *educate* industry. . . . Protectionist measures can be justified only as a means of encouraging and protecting the home manufacturing power, and only among those nations which are . . . called to secure for themselves a position equal to that of the foremost agricultural, manufacturing, and trading nations, the great maritime and continental powers.[1]

Nothing of the kind exists at present despite the assertions of some bourgeois scholars. Present-day "high protectionism" is nothing but the economic policy of the cartels as formulated by the state; present-day customs duties are cartel duties, *i.e.*, they are a means in the hands of the cartels for obtaining additional profit, for it is quite obvious that if competition is eliminated or reduced to a minimum in the home market, the "producers" can raise the prices inside the home market, adding an increment equal to the tariff. This additional profit makes it possible to sell commodities on the world market below the cost of production, to practice *dumping*, which is the peculiar export policy of the cartels. This explains the apparently strange phenomenon that present-day tariffs "protect" also export industries. Already Engels saw clearly the connection existing between the growth of cartels on the one hand and modern tariffs with their specific characteristics on the other.

The fact [he says] that the rapidly and enormously growing productive forces grow beyond the control of the laws of the capitalist mode of exchanging commodities, inside of which they are supposed to move, impresses itself nowadays more and more even on the minds of the capitalists. This is shown especially by two symptoms. First, by the new and general mania for a protective tariff, which differs from the old protectionism especially by the fact that now the articles which are *capable of being exported* are the best protected. In the second place, it is shown by the *trusts* of manufacturers of whole spheres of production.[2]

It was in our time that a gigantic stride forward was made in this direction. Consolidated industry, led by the heavy

---

[1] Friedrich List: *Gesammelte Schriften*, herausgegeben von Ludwig Häuser in 3 Teilen, Stuttgart und Tübingen, 1851. *Das nationale System der politischen Oekonomie*, pp. 302-311. [English: *The National System of Political Economy*, New York, 1904.—*Trans.*]

[2] Karl Marx: *Capital*, Vol. III, Untermann's translation, p. 142, Note 16 (by Engels). This, however, is of little aid to Prof. Josef Gruntzel, who does not understand the above-mentioned phenomena. See his *Handelspolitik*, Part IV, of *Grundriss der Wirtschaftspolitik*, p. 76. In justice, it must be noted, however, that the difference between educational and cartel duties is commonplace in economic literature, from Brentano to Hilferding. See, for instance, Josef Hellauer: *System der Welthandelslehre*, Vol. I, 1910, p. 37; Tschierschky, *l.c.*, p. 86, etc.

industries, appears as the most ardent advocate of a high tariff system, for the higher the tariff the greater is the additional profit, the easier is it to conquer new markets, and the greater is the general volume of profits obtained. The limit is reached only when the demand shrinks to such an extent that the loss is no longer compensated by the high prices. Inside of these limitations, however, the tendency to higher tariffs is an undisputed fact.

When we now survey world economy as a whole, there appears before our eyes the following picture. Cartel tariffs and the dumping system practiced by the foremost countries provoke resistance on the part of the backward countries which raise their defencive tariffs; [1] on the other hand the raising of tariffs by the backward countries serves as a further stimulus to raise the cartel duties that make dumping easier. Needless to say that the same action and counteraction take place both among the foremost countries in relation to each other and among backward countries in their mutual relations. This endless screw, perpetually applied by the growth of cartel organisations, has called forth the "tariff mania" of which Engels spoke, and which has grown even more pronounced in our days.

From the end of the seventies of the last century, there can be observed in all countries distinguished by modern development a turn from free trade to a tariff system. The latter, rapidly evolving from a system supposed to "educate" industry into a system safeguarding the cartels, finally becomes the high protectionism of our days.

In Germany this turn takes a definite form with the introduction of the tariff of 1879. Since then we see in Germany a continuous growth of tariff duties (compare, for instance, the tariff of 1902 with the later tariffs); in Austria-Hungary, the turn dates back to 1878; the subsequent tariffs reveal a similar rising tendency (particularly the tariffs of 1882, 1887, 1906, etc.); in France, a decisive turn towards protectionism was taken by the general tariff of 1881 which raised the duties on

---

[1] We must not forget that when we speak of the policies of *countries* we mean the policies of their *governments* as determined by the *social forces* on which the governments are based. Unfortunately, it is still necessary to remind one of this truth, for there are gentlemen like Mr. Plekhanov & Co., whose point of view is the "scientifically absolutely untenable 'national' point of view."

industrial imports 24 per cent; mention must be made also of the high protectionist tariff of 1892 (with duties on manufactured goods amounting to 69 per cent *ad valorem*, and on agricultural goods, 25 per cent) and its "revision" in 1910. In Spain, the tariff of 1877 already contains high duties on industrial goods; particular attention is due the tariff of 1906 with its general increase of duties. In the United States, that classical country of trusts and of the modern tariff policy, the characteristic features of protectionism are most salient. An increase of import duties begins in 1883 in connection with the growth of trusts, and reaches 40 per cent of the value of the imported goods; in 1873-74, the general duties were 38 per cent; in 1887, 47.11 per cent; in 1890 (the McKinley Bill) we have a further increase of the tariff (91 per cent on woolen goods, and even as much as 150 per cent *ad valorem* on fine grades of woolens, 40-80 per cent on metals, etc.);[1] there follow later the Dingley Bill (1897), and the Payne Tariff of 1909 which is one of the striking expressions of high protectionist tendencies. England, that citadel of free trade, is in a period of transition; there is an increasing number of ever sharper and more persistent voices demanding fair trade instead of free trade, *i.e.*, the introduction of a protectionist system (see, for instance, the activities of Chamberlain, the Imperial Federation League, and the United Empire League, etc.). A partial realisation of these tendencies is the system of preference tariffs between the mother country and the colonies. Beginning with 1898, Canada exchanged tariff privileges with England; in 1900, and again in 1906, those tariffs were developed and "improved"; at present, the privileges amount to 10-50 per cent compared with foreign countries. In 1903, the example of Canada was emulated by the South African colonies (6.25-25 per cent); in 1903, and again in 1907, New Zealand followed suit; in 1907, the Union of Australian Colonies joined (5-10 per cent). At the so-called Imperial Conferences (*i.e.*, conferences of representatives of the colonies and of the British Government) the note of pro-

---

[1] Isayev: *World Economy*, pp. 115-116. Prof. Isayev's explanation of these phenomena are unique. The raising of the tariffs in 1862-4 he explains, *e.g.*, by "the protectionist inclinations of the persons who managed American finances." He says so verbatim (pp. 114-115). See also Gruntzel, *l.c.*

tectionism becomes more clearly audible each time. "Only a second-rate thinker can be in favour of free trade at the present time and still be optimistic in relation to England," quoth with limitless bourgeois conceit the well-known economist, Aschli, thus expressing the sentiment of the English ruling classes.[1]

It is well known that the war has brought out all tendencies in the sharpest form; the tariff policy has become a fact. We must also mention the unusually high tariffs prevailing in Russia.

The new policy [says Mr. Kurchinsky] has its origin in the tariff of 1877. Since then the country is passing to higher and higher tariffs. In 1877 an increase was effected by levying the duties in gold currency, which at once raised them 40 per cent. The subsequent years brought further increases in duties levied upon a great number of commodities, thus developing the protectionist principles more and more; in 1890 all tariffs were raised 20 per cent. The movement culminates in the extremely protectionist tariff of 1891, in which the duties levied upon many commodities were increased 100-300 per cent *and even more* above the duties of 1868" [*italics ours.—N.B.*]. "The tariff now in effect was promulgated in 1903 and became effective February 16, 1906. *According to this tariff, many duties were still further increased*[2] [*italics ours.—N.B.*].

There is not the slightest doubt that we have before us a general tendency towards protecting the "national economies" by a high tariff wall. The fact that in individual cases there may be a lowering of the tariffs or mutual concessions stipulated in treaties, does not alter the general rule; all such facts are only exceptions, temporary halts, an armistice in the everlasting war. *The general tendency* is in no way disturbed by such facts, since the tendency is not a simple empirical fact, not an accidental phenomenon, not something irrelevant as regards modern relations; on the contrary, the very structure of modern capitalism gives birth to this form of economic

[1] W. J. Aschli: "La conférence impériale britannique de 1907," in *Revue économique internationale*, 1907, Vol. 4, p. 477.
[2] Kurchinsky's addenda to Prof. Eheberg's book quoted above (p. 411). As to the increase in the duties levied upon German manufactured goods in 1904, even Mr. Kurchinsky says, that "it was hardly advantageous for Russian national business" (p. 412). He thus distinguishes between business and the businessman. This *ad notam* of those who unlearn in old age.

policy; together with that structure it comes into being, and together with it it will fall.

The important economic part now played by tariffs brings about also the aggressive character of the policy of "modern capitalism." Indeed, it is due to the tariffs that monopoly organisations gather additional profit, to be utilised also as export premiums in the struggle for markets (dumping). This additional profit may grow, generally speaking, in two ways: first, through more intensive selling inside the limits of the existing state territory; second, through the growth of the latter. As regards the former, there is an obstacle here in the shape of market capacity; one cannot imagine that the big bourgeoisie would begin to increase the share of the working class, in order thus to drag itself out of the mire by the hair. Cunning businessmen that they are, they prefer to follow the other way, the way of enlarging economic territory. The greater the economic territory, other conditions being equal, the greater will be the additional profit, the easier it will be to pay export premiums and to practice dumping, the larger consequently will be the foreign sales, and the higher the rate of profit. Let us imagine that the volume of commodities prepared for export is unusually large compared with the volume that can be absorbed in the home market. Under such conditions it is impossible to compensate the losses sustained on the foreign market by the monopoly prices at home: dumping then proves senseless. On the other hand, where there is a "correct" ratio between internal sales and exports, a maximum of profits can be squeezed out. This is possible only when the internal market has a certain capacity, which, assuming demand to be equal, is determined by the size of the territory included within the tariff walls, *i.e.*, the state boundaries. While in former times, in the era of free competition, it was sufficient simply to penetrate the foreign market with commodities, and such economic occupation satisfied the capitalists of the exporting country, in our era the interests of finance capital demand, first of all, an expansion of the home state territory, *i.e.*, it dictates a policy of conquest, a pressure of military force, a line of "imperialist annexation." It is perfectly clear, however, that wherever the old liberal system of free trade has been preserved to a considerable degree in consequence of a special combination of historic conditions, and where on the other hand the state territory is sufficiently large, there we have, together with the policy of conquest, a tendency towards combining the disunited parts of the state organism, towards fusing the colonies with the metropolis, towards forming a vast single empire with a general tariff wall. Such is the policy of English imperialism. There is nothing behind the discussions about the creation of a middle European tariff alliance but the wish to create a vast economic territory as a monopoly system allowing more successful competition on the external market. In reality this is a product of the interests and the ideology of finance capitalism which, penetrating into all the pores of world economy, creates at the same time an unusually strong tendency towards secluding the national organisms, towards economic autarchy as a means of strengthening the monopoly situation of the respective capitalist groups. Thus, together with the internationalisation of economy and the internationalisation of capital, there is going on a process of "national" intertwining of capital, a process of "nationalising" capital, fraught with the greatest consequences.[1]

This process of "nationalisation" of capital, *i.e.*, the creation of homogeneous economic organisms included within state boundaries and sharply opposing each other, is also stimulated by changes taking place in the three large spheres of world economy: the sphere of markets for the sale of commodities, the sphere of markets for raw materials, and the sphere of capital investment. From these three points of view we must analyse the changes that are taking place in the conditions of the reproduction of world capital.

[1] When we speak of "national" capital, "national" economy, we have in mind, here as elsewhere, not the element of nationality in the strict sense of the word, but the territorial state conception of economic life.

CHAPTER V

World Sales Markets and Changed Sales Conditions

1. MASS PRODUCTION AND OVERSTEPPING OF STATE BOUNDARIES.
2. PRICE FORMATION UNDER CONDITIONS OF EXCHANGE BETWEEN
COUNTRIES WITH DIFFERENT ECONOMIC STRUCTURES, AND FORMA-
TION OF SUPER-PROFIT. 3. COLONIAL POLICY OF GREAT POWERS, AND
DIVISION OF THE WORLD. 4. TARIFF POLICY OF POWERS, AND SALES
MARKETS. 5. SHARPENING OF COMPETITION IN WORLD SALES MARKET,
AND CAPITALIST EXPANSION.

EVERY "national" capitalism has always manifested a tendency to expand, to widen the scope of its power, to overstep
the boundaries of the nation, the state. This follows from
the very structure of capitalist society.

The conditions of direct exploitation and those of the realisation
of surplus value are not identical. They are separated logically as
well as by time and space. The first are only limited by the productive power of society, the last by the proportional relations of
the various lines of production and by the consuming power of
society. This last named power is not determined either by the
absolute productive power nor by the absolute consuming power,
but by the consuming power based on the antagonistic conditions of
distribution, which reduce the consumption of the great mass of
the population to a variable minimum within more or less narrow
limits. The consuming power is furthermore restricted by a tendency to accumulate, the greed for an expansion of capital and a
production of surplus value on an enlarged scale. This is the law
of capitalist production. . . . The market must, therefore, be
continually extended. . . . This internal contradiction seeks to
balance itself by an expansion of the outlying fields of production.[1]

This law of mass production, which is at the same time the
law of mass overproduction, must not be understood to mean
that the overstepping of "national state boundaries" is something like an absolute necessity; this necessity is created in
the process of profit formation, and the amount of the profit

---

[1] K. Marx: *Capital*, Vol. III, Untermann's translation, pp. 286-287.

serves as the regulating principle of the whole movement. The amount of the profit depends upon the mass of commodities and the amount of profit accruing to one commodity unit, which amount is equal to the selling price minus production cost. If we use for the volume of commodities the letter V, for the price of a commodity unit the letter P, and for the cost of production per unit of commodity the letter C, we find that the sum total of the profit is expressed by the formula $V(P-C)$. The smaller the production cost, the lager will be the profits per unit of commodity, and, assuming the sales market to be stationary or growing, the larger will be the volume of profit. The cost of production, however, is the lower, the greater the volume of commodities brought into the market. Improved methods of production, expansion of productive forces, and consequently increase in the volume of goods produced, are factors decreasing the cost of production. This explains the selling of commodities abroad at low prices. Even if such sales yield no profits at all, even if the commodities are sold at production cost, the volume of profit is still increased, since thus the cost of production is made lower. (We do not speak here of sales made at a loss for "strategic purposes," *i.e.*, for a rapid conquest of the market and for the annihilation of the competitors.) In the general formula $V(P-C)$, the volume of production costs will not be that amount which corresponds to the volume of goods designated as V, but a much smaller amount corresponding to the formula $V+E$, where E is understood to be the amount of exported commodities. It is in this way that the movement of profits compels commodities to overstep the boundaries of state. The very same regulating principle of capitalism—rate of profit—acts in still another way. We have in mind the formation of super-profit under the conditions of commodity exchange between countries having different economic structures.

Even in the epoch of commercial capital this process of the formation of additional profit is perfectly clear.

So long as merchants' capital [says Marx] promotes the exchange of products between undeveloped societies, commercial profit does not only assume the shape of outbargaining and cheating, but also arises largely from these methods. Leaving aside the fact that it exploits the difference in the prices of production of the various countries . . . those modes of production bring it about that merchants' capital appropriates to itself the overwhelming portion of the surplus product, either in its capacity as a mediator between societies, which are as yet largely engaged in the production of use-value for whose economic organisation the sale of that portion of its product which is transferred to the circulation, or any sale of products at their value, is of minor importance; or, because under those former modes of production the principal owners of the surplus product, with whom the merchant has to deal, are the slave owner, the feudal landlord, the state . . . and they represent the wealth and luxury.[1]

In these conditions "outbargaining" and "cheating" were able to play such an important part because the process of exchange was irregular, because it was not the necessary process of "metabolism" in a society with a world wide division of labour; on the contrary, it was a more or less accidental phenomenon. However, additional profit is obtained also at a time when the international exchange of commodities already becomes a regularly recurring moment in the reproduction of world capital. Marx gave a complete explanation of the economic nature of this super-profit in the following statements:

Capitals invested in foreign trade are in a position to yield a higher rate of profit, because, in the first place, they come in competition with commodities produced in other countries with lesser facilities of production, so that an advanced country is enabled to sell its goods above their value even when it sells them cheaper than the competing countries. To the extent that the labour of the advanced countries is here exploited as labour of a higher specific weight, the rate of profit rises, because labour which has not been paid as being of a higher quality is sold as such. The same condition may obtain in the relations with a certain country, into which commodities are exported or from which commodities are imported. This country may offer more materialised labour in goods than it receives, and yet it may receive in return commodities cheaper than it could produce them. In the same way a manufacturer, who exploits a new invention before it has become general, undersells his competitors and yet sells his commodities above their individual values, that is to say, he exploits the specifically higher productive power of the labour employed by him as surplus value. *By this*

[1] *Ibid.*, p. 389.

means he secures a surplus profit [*italics ours.—N.B.*]; on the
other hand, capitals invested in colonies, etc., may yield a higher
rate of profit for the simple reason that the rate of profit is higher
there on account of the backward development, and for the added
reason that slaves, coolies, etc., permit a better exploitation of
labour. We see no reason why these higher rates of profit realised
by capitals invested in certain lines and sent home by them should
not enter as elements into the average rate of profit and tend to
keep it to that extent.[1]

Marx, proceeding from the theory of labour value, gives here
an explanation of super-profits. From this point of view,
additional profit has its source in the difference between the
social value of the goods (understanding under "society"
world capitalism as a united whole) and their individual value
(understanding under "individual" the "national economy").
Furthermore, Marx foresaw and explained cases where a certain *fixation* of additional profit goes on, namely when a certain
territory is dominated by monopoly organisations—cases that
are particularly important in our times.

It is thus obvious that not the impossibility of doing business at home, but the race for higher rates of profit is the
motive power of world capitalism. Even present-day "capitalist plethora" is no absolute limit. A lower rate of profit
drives commodities and capital further and further from their
"home." This process is going on simultaneously in various
sections of world economy. The capitalists of various "national economies" clash here as competitors; and the more
vigorous the expansion of the productive forces of world
capitalism, the more intensive the growth of foreign trade, the
sharper is the competitive struggle. During the last decades
quantitative changes of such magnitude have taken place in
this realm that the very quality of the phenomenon has assumed a new form.

Those changes proceed, so to speak, from two ends. On
the one hand, the process of mass production is becoming
extremely accelerated, *i.e.*, the volume of commodities seeking
for a foreign market is increasing—a phenomenon highly characteristic of recent times; on the other hand, the free market,
i.e., that section of it which has not been seized by the "great

[1] *Ibid.*, p. 279.

power" monopolies, becomes ever narrower. Moved by the requirements of home capital, the great powers very quickly subjugated the free territories; beginning from 1870-1880 the process of "territorial acquisitions" went on at a feverish tempo. For our purposes it is sufficient to give a brief account of the results of the "colonial policy" which has become a veritable mania of all modern capitalist states.

England, a country with a vast state territory, has, after 1870, succeeded in annexing a whole series of new territories: Baluchistan, Burma, Cyprus, British North Borneo, Wei-hai-Wei, the territories adjoining Hongkong in Asia; it increased the Straits Settlements; it took Koweit under its protectorate (1899); it acquired the Sinai peninsula, etc.; it annexed some islands in Australia, also the southeastern part of New Guinea, the major portion of the Solomon Islands, and the Tonga Islands. In Africa, where competition and seizures were going on with particular intensity, England acquired Egypt, the Egyptian part of Sudan with Uganda, British East Africa, British Somali, Zanzibar, and Pemba; in Southern Africa, the two Boer republics, Rhodesia, British Central Africa; in Western Africa, outside of increasing the former colonies, it occupied Nigeria.[1] Such were the "successes" of England.

France acted no less "successfully."

Beginning with 1870 [we read in a work of a French imperialist] we witness an actual colonial regeneration. The Third Republic placed Annam under its protectorate, it conquered Tongking, it annexed Laos, it extended a French protectorate over Tunis and the Comoro Islands [near Madagascar—N.B.], it occupied Madagascar, it increased its possessions in Sahara, Sudan, Guinea, the Ivory Coast, Dagomea, the Somali coast, out of all proportions [démésurement], and it founded a new France extending from the Atlantic Ocean and Congo to Lake Chad.[2]

By the end of the nineteenth century the area of the French colonies was nineteen times the area of France proper.

German imperialism appeared later in the arena, but it made haste to regain lost time. The beginning of Germany's

[1] S. Schilder, l.c., 147 ff.
[2] Paul Gaffarel: *L'histoire de l'expansion coloniale de la France depuis 1870 jusqu'en 1915; avant-propos.*

colonial policy dates back to 1884. It conquered Southwestern Africa, Cameroon, Togoland, East Africa, it "acquired" New Guinea and a number of islands (Emperor Wilhelm's Land, "The Bismarck Archipelago," the Caroline Islands, the Marianas, etc.); in 1897 it seized Kiaochow, it made ready to grab sections of Turkey and Asia Minor—all this "evolution" being accomplished with feverish haste.[1]

As to the Russian colonial policy, we wish to remind the readers of the conquest of Central Asia, of the Russian policy in Manchuria and Mongolia, and lately in Persia, the latter being accomplished with the aid of England (Colonel Liakhov is its hero).[2] The same policies are pursued also by countries in other hemispheres, the most important of which are the United States and Japan. In consequence of this "division" of free lands, and with them, to a large extent, of free markets, world competition among the "national" capitalist groups was bound to become exceedingly sharpened. The present distribution of territories and populations is illustrated by the following table:

COLONIAL POSSESSIONS OF THE GREAT POWERS
(In millions of square kilometers and in millions of inhabitants)

| | COLONIES | | | | "HOME" | | TOTALS | |
| | 1876 | | 1914 | | 1914 | | 1914 | |
	Area	Pop.	Area	Pop.	Area	Pop.	Area	Pop.
Britain	22.5	251.9	33.5	393.5	.3	46.5	33.8	440.0
Russia	17.0	15.9	17.4	33.2	5.4	136.2	22.8	169.4
France	.9	6.0	10.6	55.5	.5	39.6	11.1	95.1
Germany	....	2.9	12.3	.5	64.9	3.4	77.2
U. S. A.	....	.3	9.7	9.4	97.0	9.7	106.7
Japan	....	.3	19.2	.4	53.0	.7	72.2
Total ...	40.4	273.8	65.0	523.4	16.5	437.2	81.5	960.6

Colonies of other powers (Belgium, Holland, etc.)		9.9	45.3
Semi-colonial countries (Persia, China, Turkey)		14.5	361.2
Other countries		28.0	289.9
Total Area and Population of the World		133.9	1657.0[3]

[1] B. von König: "Le développement commercial, économique et financier des colonies allemandes," in *Revue économique internationale,* 1907, Vol. 4, p. 130.

[2] M. N. Pokrovsky, "Russia's Foreign Policy at the End of the Nineteenth Century," in his *History of Russia in the Nineteenth Century.*

[3] The table was compiled by Comrade V. Ilyin [V. I. Lenin] and is quoted from one of his recent works. [*Imperialism As the Final Stage of Capitalism.*]

Thus between 1876 and 1914 the great powers acquired about 25 million square kilometers of colonial lands, in area twice the size of Europe. All the world is divided among the "economies" of the great nations. This explains why competition is becoming unbelievably sharp, why the pressure of capitalist expansion on the remaining free lands increases in the same ratio as the chances for a grandiose free for all among the large capitalist powers.[1]

The tariffs only tend to increase such chances. The tariffs are barriers that stand in the way of the import of commodities; they can be overcome in one way only: through pressure, through the use of force. Tariff wars are sometimes practiced, as a preliminary, *i.e.*, rates are increased in order to extort concessions. Such tariff wars, for instance, were waged by Austria-Hungary against Roumania (1886-1890), Serbia (1906-1911), Montenegro (1908-1911); by Germany against Russia (1893-1894), Spain (1894-1899), and Canada (1903-1910); by France against Italy (1888-1892) and Switzerland (1893-1895), etc. The quicker the free markets are "distributed," the quicker are they included within the tariff walls; and the more ferocious competition becomes, the sharper are the tariff clashes between great powers. Tariff wars, however, are only partial sorties, they are only a sort of testing the ground. In the long run the conflict is solved by the interrelation of "real forces," *i.e.*, by the force of arms. Thus the race for sales markets inevitably creates conflicts between the "national groups of capital." The enormous increase in the productive forces, coupled with the shrinking to a minimum of free markets in recent times; the tariff policy of the powers, connected as it is with the rule of finance capital, and the mounting difficulties for realising commodity values—all this creates a situation where the last word belongs to military technique.

The contradictions of capitalist development, as analysed by Marx, become apparent. The growth of productive forces

---

[1] This is why, beginning from 1871, all international conflicts are caused by colonial policy. See Ioaquin Fernández Prida: *Historia de los conflictos internacionales del siglo XIX*, Barcelona, 1901, p. 118 *ff*. That the expansion policy is directed in the first place towards the free territories is explained by the tendency of the bourgeoisie to follow the line of least resistance.

clashes with the antagonistic form of distribution and with the disproportion between the various parts of capitalist production—hence capital expansion; on the other hand, socialised labour clashes with the organisation of capital as private business, which expresses itself in competition between national capitalisms.   Equilibrium and a harmonious development of all parts of the social mechanism are lacking; in recent times more so than at any other; hence terrific crises and precipitous changes.

CHAPTER VI

World Market for Raw Materials, and Change in the Conditions of Purchasing Materials

1. DISPROPORTION BETWEEN PARTS OF SOCIAL PRODUCTION. 2. MONOPOLY OWNERSHIP OF LAND, AND GROWTH OF DISPROPORTION BETWEEN INDUSTRY AND AGRICULTURE. 3. DEARTH OF RAW MATERIALS, AND CONTRACTION OF THE MARKET FOR RAW MATERIALS. 4. SHARPENING OF COMPETITION IN THE WORLD MARKET FOR RAW MATERIALS, AND CAPITALIST EXPANSION.

WE have seen in the last chapter how recent developments in capitalism, making it more and more difficult to realise commodity values, force the ruling classes of the various "national" groups to embrace the policy of expansion. The reproduction process of capital is not limited, however, to the phase of sale alone. In the reproduction formula M-C . . . P . . . C'-M' only the latter part expresses the realisation of the price of the product (C'-M'). As a rule, only the difficulties inherent in the process C'-M', *i.e.*, in the process of sale, are stressed. The race for sales markets, and the industrial crises in particular, have induced the economists to analyse the difficulties met by capital when passing through the phase C'-M'. Difficulties, however, may arise also in the first phase, namely, when money is exchanged for means of production (M-C). It is a fact that the recent development of capitalist relations creates ever growing difficulties also in this sphere of the reproduction of social capital.

It is well known that the operation M-C consists of two parts: M-L and M-MP, where L signifies labour power and MP signifies means of production, so that in its developed form the formula reads M-C(L-MP). We have to examine each part of the formula separately.

In so far as the growth of productive forces has called forth changes in the structure of society and in the interrelation of class forces, it has expressed itself, among other things, in the fact that social antagonisms become exceedingly sharp, that the organised forces of class opponents face each other squarely. The state of apparent equilibrium here implies an extraordinary pressure of social forces upon one another. The tendency towards lowering the rate of profit calls forth the tendency to intensify labour on the one hand, to seek for cheap hands and a long labour day on the other. The latter, too, is achieved in the sphere of colonial policy.[1]

The other side of the issue, however, is of still greater importance.

We have in mind the disproportion between the development of industry and the development of agriculture as a source of raw material for the manufacturing industry. The latter requires greater and greater volumes of raw materials, namely wood (paper industry, building trades, cabinet making, railroad construction, etc.), animal products (hides, wool, bristles, horsehair, furs, bones, intestines, animal fats of all sorts, meat as material for the manufacturing of foods, etc.), raw materials for the textile industry (cotton, flax, hemp, etc.), finally such commodities as rubber, which plays a colossal part in all phases of industrial life, etc. The development of agriculture, however, does not keep pace with the impetuous development of industry, hence, as a fundamental fact, the high prices which have become an international phenomenon of prime importance, particularly in the recent period of capitalist development, when the industrial process has become so rapid that even the production of agriculture on the other side of the ocean could not keep pace any longer with the demand of the foremost capitalist countries for agricultural products, and the fall of world prices was followed by their rapid rise. The table below gives some idea as to the rise of prices of different commodities.

Within one decade (1903-1913) the jute price rose 128 per cent, that of cotton 13 per cent, that of cow hides 55 per cent, of calf hides 25 per cent, of bacon 31 per cent.[2]

---

[1] We shall not dwell here on the methods of exploitation with which this policy has besmirched itself. We only call attention to the fact that it is not all in the "past," that, to a large degree, it is also in the present.

[2] On the relation between industry and agriculture as expressed in high prices, see a small but excellent pamphlet by Otto Bauer, *Die Teuerung*.

PRICE IN RUBLES PER POOD

Years	Raw Jute on London Market	Raw Cotton	Salted Hides	Russian Calf Hides	American Bacon
			HAMBURG MARKET		
1903	1.77	9.12	6.11	19.62	6.62
1904	1.76	9.57	6.49	20.93	5.57
1905	2.42	7.72	6.93	28.64	5.79
1906	3.04	8.96	7.90	28.82	6.31
1907	2.51	9.87	7.96	27.90	7.07
1908	1.88	8.47	6.52	28.65	7.01
1909	1.83	9.46	7.22	25.38	8.97
1910	1.98	11.72	8.35	27.33	9.52
1911	2.62	10.51	8.40	26.54	7.04
1912	2.86	9.65	8.57	25.50	8.17
1913	3.93	10.35	9.47	24.60	8.66 [1]

It is true that under all circumstances, and even in a socialised society, the development of the productive forces would tend towards the production of means of production. (We have seen that in capitalist society this process assumes the form of a higher organic composition of capital.) But under normal conditions this would not mean a disproportion in the distribution of the productive forces of society. On the contrary, the course of development would be smooth and harmonious, the "demand" for raw materials growing as rapidly as their "supply." What matters here is not the relative growth of industry in general, but the disproportion in the growth of its various parts. On the other hand, this course of development must not be looked upon as the expression of an "absolute" and "natural" law, which hampers the development of agricultural products in the manner pictured by Malthus and by his numerous avowed and secret followers. The main obstacle here lies in a special social category—the monopoly of land ownership.

[1] *List of Prices in Principal Russian and Foreign Markets for 1913,* published by the Ministry of Commerce and Industry, Petrograd, 1914.

The mere legal property in land [says Marx in his chapter on absolute ground-rent] does not create any ground-rent for the landlord. But it gives him the power to withdraw his land from exploitation until the economic conditions permit him to utilise it in such a way that it will yield him a surplus whenever the land is used either for agriculture proper or for other productive purposes, such as buildings, etc. He cannot increase or decrease the absolute quantity of its field of employment, but he can do so with its marketable quantity. For this reason, as Fourier has already remarked, a characteristic fact in all civilised countries is that a comparatively considerable portion of the land always remains uncultivated.[1]

Private property in land is then the barrier which does not permit any new investment of capital upon hitherto uncultivated or un-rented land without levying a tax, in other words, without demanding a rent, although the land to be taken under new cultivation may belong to a class which does not produce any differential rent, [i.e., rent obtained in consequence of the difference in the quality of the pieces of land, etc.—N.B.] and which, were it not for the inter-vention of private property in land, might have been cultivated at a small increase in the market price, so that the regulating market price would have netted to the cultivator of this worst soil nothing but his price of production [i.e., production cost plus average profit—N.B.] [2]

The difference between agriculture and manufacturing is this, that while the rise of prices for the products of the manu-facturing industry ordinarily entails a shrinking of the demand, so that the demand curve changes rapidly in accordance with the fluctuation of prices, the demand in the sphere of distri-bution of agricultural products remains comparatively more stable. (One must not forget that the production of raw materials for the manufacturing industry is in a great number of cases a by-product of the production of foodstuffs, such as the production of hides, of intestines, partly of wool, etc., being connected with the meat packing industry.) This is why competition plays a substantially smaller part in agriculture, notwithstanding the fact that monopoly organisations in the strict sense of the word are very little developed there. The laws of mass production, of an accelerated accumulation of

[1] Capital, Vol. III, pp. 878-879.
[2] Ibid., pp. 884-885.

capital, etc., apply to agriculture much less than to industry.

Thus to the disproportion between the branches of production of capitalist economy in general, as emanating from the anarchical economic structure of capitalism and continuing to exist despite the processes of cartelisation, trustification, etc., there is added the specific and ever growing disproportion between industry and agriculture. It is not surprising that this latter disproportion has become most pronounced in recent times. We have noted above the intensive growth of productive forces in the last decade. The trans-oceanic countries, in the first place the United States, have developed their own industry, and consequently their own demand for an ever growing amount of agricultural products. The same took place in other agrarian countries. In Austria-Hungary, for instance, the import of breadstuffs, etc., outgrew their export in a very short time. The general rise of the productive forces of world capitalism in the last decade has so shifted and changed the interrelation between industrial and agricultural production that here, too, quantitative changes have reached a point beyond which qualitative changes begin. This is why the epoch of dearth, of a general rise in the prices of agricultural products everywhere, is a phenomenon of the most recent phase of capitalism The rise in the prices of raw materials in turn reveals itself directly in the rate of profit, for, other conditions being equal, the rate of profit rises and falls in inverse ratio to the fluctuations in the prices of raw material. Hence a growing tendency on the part of the capitalists of the individual "national economies" to widen their markets for raw materials. The same process, however, which caused the sales markets to shrink immensely, affected in like manner the markets for raw materials, since the markets for raw materials have been, and are, mainly the same countries that serve as a "foreign" market for the sale of manufactured goods, *i.e.*, the countries of a lower development, including the colonies. The interests of the capitalists of the various great powers clash here as strongly as in the competition in the sphere of sales. There is nothing surprising in this since the process of the reproduction of social capital presupposes the importance not only of those changes that may take place in the last phase of the circulation chain, M-C . . . P . . . C′-M′, *i.e.*, in the phase of sale, but also of those that may take place in the phase M-L, *i.e.*, in the phase of purchasing means of production. A capitalist "producer" is not only a vendor but also a buyer. He is not a vendor and a buyer pure and simple, but a capitalist vendor and a capitalist buyer; the acts of buying and selling are included here in the formula of capital circulation. They are parts of that formula. Hence it is perfectly obvious that Franz Oppenheimer's theory concerning the "peaceful character" of the buyers' competition and the hostile relations between vendors is entirely artificial.[1] He takes as a basis for his argument the thesis that the vendor ordinarily brings into the market only one commodity, and that his fate is connected with that commodity alone, *i.e.*, with its price, whereas, says Oppenheimer, "the buyer is interested in a great variety of goods and their prices, and his interests depend comparatively little upon each one of those commodities since the price of one commodity may rise while the price of the other falls," etc. Oppenheimer fails to realise the most essential point, namely, that a present-day buyer is largely a *capitalist* buyer. Personal consumption is relegated to the rear compared with productive consumption on the basis of a widening reproduction. For production purposes, however, a mass purchase of a comparatively small number of commodities is required. As a rule, large masses of staple goods are being purchased, and *one* commodity often plays a highly important part. (Compare the importance of cotton for the textile industry.) [2]

Thus there are no reasons why we should consider the struggle for raw material less acute, as Oppenheimer would wish us to do. The immense growth of competition in this field is a fact which takes on still greater significance due to

[1] See his reasoning on the causes of the war in *Die Neue Rundschau,* August, 1915 (Franz Oppenheimer: "Die Wurzel des Krieges"). His general view concerning the course of social development, and his "positive solution of the problem," which, in our opinion, do not go far beyond the views of Henry George and the bourgeois "land reformists," are expounded in his "critical" work entitled, *Die Soziale Frage und der Sozialismus,* Jena, 1912. No one but Mr. P. Maslov is under the strong influence of this economist.

[2] Even the "producers" *in concreto* produce more than one commodity, not to speak of vendors in general. Department stores are a case in point. By this we do not mean to deny the importance of specialisation. We only wish to rehabilitate the "besmirched reputation" of the buyers.

the tendency of annexing territories containing deposits of coal, iron ore, copper ore, oil deposits, etc. Branches of industry that play an enormous rôle and that depend on natural conditions, are easily monopolised, and once they have fallen into the hands of certain "national" groups, they are lost for the others. Of course, this applies also to agricultural production in so far as there appears on the arena a consolidated "national" group which has at its disposal the means of "occupation." England's policy in Egypt, the transformation of all of Egypt into a gigantic cotton plantation furnishing raw material for the English textile industry, may serve as a striking illustration.

It follows that the recent phase of capitalism sharpens the conflicts also in this sphere. The faster the tempo of capitalist development, the stronger the process of industrialisation of the economic life and urbanisation of the country, the more disturbed is the equilibrium between industry and agriculture, the stronger is the competition between industrially developed countries for the possession of backward countries, the more unavoidable becomes an open conflict between them.

Here, too, capitalist expansion is a "way out" of contradictions that leads with impeccable logic to the decisive moment of imperialist policy—*war*.

We have so far analysed the changes that have taken place within the conditions of the world circulation of commodities and which have extraordinarily sharpened the competition between "national" capitalisms, and consequently also their aggressive policy. However, the changes that characterise our epoch are not confined to these spheres alone. The development of the productive forces of world capitalism has brought to the fore other forms of international economic relations. We have in mind the international movement of capital values, which we shall presently analyse.

CHAPTER VII

World Movement of Capital, and Change in the Economic Forms of International Connections

1. OVERPRODUCTION OF CAPITAL AND ITS GROWTH. 2. MOVING FORCES OF CAPITAL EXPORT. 3. CARTELS AND CAPITAL EXPORT. 4. CAPITAL EXPORT AND LOANS. 5. CAPITAL EXPORT AND COMMERCIAL TREATIES. 6. CAPITAL EXPORT AND COMMODITY EXPORT. 7. SHARPENING OF COMPETITION FOR CAPITAL INVESTMENT SPHERES; CAPITALIST EXPANSION.

THE international movement of capital may be looked upon from the point of view of the country that exports, or from the point of view of the country that imports capital.

The export of capital from a country presupposes an overproduction of capital in that country, an overaccumulation of capital. The overproduction would be absolute were the increment of capital to yield nothing from the capitalist point of view, namely, if capital, C, having increased to $C + \triangle C$, were to yield as much profit as it would without the increment $\triangle C$.[1] For the export of capital, however, it is not necessary that overproduction should have reached that limit. "If capital is sent to foreign countries, it is not done because there is absolutely no employment to be had for it at home. It is done because it can be employed at a higher rate of profit in a foreign country."[2] It is therefore easy to understand why we observe capital export almost throughout the history of the development of capitalism. However, it is only in the last decades that capital export has acquired an extraordinary significance, the like of which it never had before. The specific weight of this form of international economic intercourse has so increased, that to a certain degree we may even speak of a new type of economic interrelationship between countries.

Two sets of causes have been and are operating here. In the first place, the accumulation of capital proceeds with an un-

[1] *Capital*, Vol. III, p. 295.
[2] *Ibid.*, p. 300.

usually rapid tempo, due to large-scale capitalist production accompanied by incessant technical progress which makes gigantic strides and increases the productive power of labour, and to the unusual increase in the means of transportation and the perfection of means of circulation in general, which also hastens the turn-over of capital. The volumes of capital that seek employment have reached unheard of dimensions. On the other hand, the cartels and trusts, as the modern organisation of capital, tend to put certain limits to the employment of capital by fixing the volume of production. As to the non-trustified sections of industry, it becomes ever more unprofitable to invest capital in them. For monopoly organisations can overcome the tendency towards lowering the rate of profit by receiving monopoly superprofits at the expense of the non-trustified industries. Out of the surplus value created every year, one portion, that which has been created in the non-trustified branches of industry, is being transferred to the co-owners of capitalist monopolies, whereas the share of the outsiders continually decreases. Thus the entire process drives capital beyond the frontiers of the country.

In the second place, high tariffs put tremendous obstacles in the way of commodities seeking to enter a foreign country. Mass production and mass overproduction make the growth of foreign trade necessary, but foreign trade meets with a barrier in the form of high tariffs. It is true that foreign trade keeps on developing, foreign sales grow, but this is taking place notwithstanding the difficulties and in spite of them. This does not mean, however, that the tariffs do not make themselves felt. Their influence is, first of all, expressed in the rate of profit. Tariff barriers, making the export of commodities very difficult, do not interfere in any way with the export of capital. Obviously, the higher the wave of duties, the larger, other conditions being equal, is the flight of capital from its home country.

The protection of industry [!] does not stimulate foreigners to establish a factory inside the tariff frontiers. Only when the foreign manufacturer and importer has lost part or all of his sales, does a moment arrive when he resorts to the establishment of factories in foreign countries—an undertaking always connected with great expense and risks. Prohibitive tariffs bringing about such consequences are contained in the McKinley and Dingley Bills of the U. S. (1890 and 1897); in the Russian legislation of 1877, 1881, 1885, and 1891; also in the French laws of 1881 and 1892.[1]

Tariff duties influence capital export also in another way. They themselves become an attraction for a capitalist. In so far as capital has been imported and begins to function in a "foreign" country as capital, it receives as much "protection" from the tariff as the capital of native businessmen.[2] This in turn causes a tremendous increase in capital export.

Capital export, however, must not be taken *per se,* without any connection with other highly important economic and political phenomena accompanying it. Let us glance at a few of the most significant of those phenomena.

In case of state or municipal loans, the creditor country receives more than interest on the sums advanced. The transaction is usually accompanied by a number of stipulations, in the first place that which imposes upon the borrowing country the duty to place orders with the creditor country (purchase of arms, ammunition, dreadnaughts, railroad equipment, etc.), and the duty to grant concessions for the construction of railways, tramways, telegraph and telephone lines, harbours, exploitation of mines, timberlands, etc. Such transactions are either included in the loan contract as one of its conditions, or they are an inevitable consequence of the entire "course of events." As an example we quote here a description of one of the concessions granted by the Persian government to the (Russian) Discount and Loan Bank of Persia for the construction of the railway line Julfa-Tabriz (1913):

The line gage is Russian. The time of concession is 75 years. The Persian government has the option of redeeming the railroad after the expiration of 35 years; in this case it pays back all the capital that has been spent plus 5 per cent interest, provided the concession has yielded so much. The concession grants the bank the right to exploit coal and oil deposits within 60 versts on either side of the railroad, and also to construct branch lines leading to the mines. The bank also obtains the preference right to construct the railway line Tabriz-Kazoin, and the exclusive right to

[1] Sartorius von Waltershausen, *l.c.,* p. 179.
[2] *Ibid.,* p. 180.

construct a turnpike between the same points within eight years, also the right to exploit coal and oil deposits within 60 versts on either side of the road. After deducting from the profits of the railroad in favour of the concessionaire 7 per cent on all capital spent on its construction, the remaining net income is divided equally between the concessionaire and the Persian government. As to the oil and coal mines, the concessionaire pays to the Persian government 5 per cent of the net profits obtained from them. All the concessionaire's enterprises are free of taxes and other duties for all times.[1]

Among the "measures" intended to restrict foreign capital we find the right of the governmental power to prohibit the quotation of foreign loans and securities in general. Thus by a special law dated February 6, 1880, the French Ministry of Finance was empowered to prohibit the traffic in foreign securities, also to refuse foreign loans to be quoted in the French stock exchanges (in 1909 the French government refused to grant a loan to Argentina because in 1908 the latter had placed an order with Krupp and not with Schneider in Creuzot; in 1909, the same government refused to grant a loan to Bulgaria for lack of sufficient guarantees—the loan was secured by an Austro-German bank syndicate; for four decades German securities were not allowed to be quoted in France; in September, 1910, a loan was refused to Hungary; a loan was granted Serbia under the condition of placing orders with Schneider; after the Revolution, the Russian Government ordered cruisers to be constructed in France in return for loans, etc.).[2]

Aside from orders and concessions, definite advantages in regard to trade treaties may be secured together with the loan contract. (See, for instance, the Russo-French trade treaty of September 16-29, 1905, which was prolonged to 1917; the treaty of December 2, 1908, between Sweden and France; the treaty of 1908 between Sweden and Denmark; the tariff treaty of August 19, 1911, between France and Japan; compare also the refusal of France to allow the shares of the United States Steel Corporation to be quoted on the Paris exchange in retali-

[1] M. P. Pavlovich: *The Great Railway and Maritime Lines of the Future*, St. Petersburg, 1913, p. 143.
[2] S. Schilder, *l.c.*, p. 343 ff.

ation for duties imposed on wine, silk, and automobiles by the Payne Tariff of America in 1909.[1]

When capital is exported by private persons or by industrial and banking companies, this again increases the export of commodities from the motherland, for the enterprises thus created abroad represent a certain demand by themselves, and besides, they widen by their very activities the market that is mostly dependent upon them. One must bear in mind that "foreign" enterprises are, as we have seen in the first section, financed by the largest banks or bank trusts and are possessed of a colossal economic power.[2] Here is one example. One-third of the land in the German colony of Cameroon is private property, but a very considerable part of this land belongs to two companies only: the South Cameroon Company holds 7,700,000 hectares, the Southwestern Cameroon Company, 8,800,000 hectares, an area six times the size of the kingdom of Saxony (1,500,000 hectares) and larger than Bavaria (7,-600,000 hectares).[3] Wherever the capitalists do not possess territory, they possess other forms of financial power. In constructing the Bagdad railroad, the Deutsche Bank not only uses German material in Turkey, but it also creates a whole network of market relations, making it easy for German goods to penetrate Turkey. Thus capital export creates favourable conditions also for the industry of its home country.

Capital export unusually sharpens the relations between the great powers. Already the struggle for opportunities to invest capital, *i.e.*, the struggle for concessions, etc., is always reinforced by military pressure. A government or a "country" subjected to the manipulations of the financiers of the great powers ordinarily yields to that party which appears to be the strongest militarily. When some pacifists (particularly their English brand) try to influence the ruling classes by logical reasons, when they try to persuade them to disarm on the ground that commodities are supposed to find a market inde-

[1] *Ibid.*, p. 353.
[2] Pavlovich cites a number of examples of how the banks act in the realm of railway construction; they actually allow entire countries to be swallowed by capitalist sharks.
[3] Compare with a highly curious book entitled, *Deutsche Colonialpolitik*, 2nd, part, *Staatsstreich oder Reformen*. The author hides under the pseudonym Ein Ausland-Deutscher, Zurich, 1905, p. 1318.

pendently of the number of dreadnaughts, they will be cruelly disappointed. For the "peaceful" policies that were pursued before the war, and will be pursued after it, were always and everywhere reinforced by the threats of military power. To use a correct expression of the Englishman Brailsford, "the continuous war of steel and gold never ceases for a minute even in peace time." More graphically is this atmosphere of obdurate competition described by an eminent theoretician of German imperialism, Sartorius:

The growing industrialisation of the world is a fact to be reckoned with by every policy of world economy [*jede Weltwirtschaftspolitik*]. . . . It is given to nobody to stop the course of development, and if a state would prohibit its subjects from establishing enterprises in other countries, this would only bring advantages to the businessmen of a third state. It is therefore best of all to have your finger in the pie in due time [*die Hand rechtzeitig im Spiele haben*]. . . . The economic world does not stand still. One change precipitates another. There is always an opportunity for a strong nation to mix in. Here, too, the slogan *"Carpe diem"* is to be applied.[1]

If the pressure of military power yields concessions and various privileges, the further functioning of capital abroad also demands specific "protection." Formerly the centre of gravity lay in commodity export, whereby the exporters risked only their goods, *i.e.*, their circulating capital. Now the situation is totally different. What we have in a "foreign" country are large sums of money, particularly of fixed capital, invested in gigantic constructions: railroads stretching over thousands of miles, very costly electric plants, large plantations, etc., etc. The capitalists of the exporting country are materially interested in "guarding" their wealth. They are therefore ready to go the limit in order that they may retain the freedom of further accumulation.[2]

[1] Sartorius von Waltershausen, *l.c.*, pp. 190-191.
[2] "Capital is said by a Quarterly Reviewer to fly turbulence and strife, and to be timid, which is very true; but this is very incompletely stating the question. Capital eschews no profit, or very small profit, just as nature was formerly said to abhor a vacuum. With adequate profit, capital is very bold. A certain 10 per cent will ensure its employment anywhere; 20 per cent certain will produce eagerness; 50 per cent, positive audacity; 100 per cent will make it ready to trample on all human law; 300 per cent, and there is not a crime at which it will scruple, nor a risk it will not run, even to the chance of its owner being hanged." P. J. Dunning, quoted by Marx, *Capital*, Vol. I, note to p. 843.

Where the exploited country is weak also militarily, "peaceful penetration" of capital very quickly turns into "peaceful occupation" or division, or else it entails an armed struggle between countries competing for capital investment spheres. The fate of Turkey in the light of Franco-German competition is very typical in this respect. We wish to quote, in illustration, the writings of one French and one German imperialist published long before the war. "The Turkish Empire has been overrun by German hordes" (*hordes germaniques*) "of traders and salesmen," says the Frenchman.

Thus the network of German banks gradually spreads over the entire Ottoman Empire, supporting industry, seizing transport facilities, competing with foreign financial institutions . . . in brief, those banks, *with powerful political support* [*italics ours—N.B.*] strive financially to establish German influence over the entire Levant.[1]

Thus a French bourgeois expresses indignation over the "German hordes." But a German bourgeois is indignant in the very same way:

The French are systematically striving to make Turkey their slave debtor; up to the present they have advanced her two billion two hundred million francs. Of this sum, one-half billion was invested in railroads alone, France having constructed more railroads than any other nation. The most important Turkish harbours, like Constantinople, Salonika, Smyrna, Beirut, are in French hands. The lighthouses along the Turkish coast are in French hands. Last but not least, the most important bank of Turkey, the Ottoman Bank, operates in Constantinople entirely under French influence. Who then can escape the political consequences of such a powerful pressure of capital! French diplomacy very intensively utilises its privileged position in Turkey, particularly in recent times![2]

Obviously, capital export in its present volume and importance is caused by the peculiarities of economic development in recent years. Looked upon from the point of view of the

[1] Dubief: "Le chemin de fer de Bagdad," in *Revue économique internationale*, 1912, Vol. 2, p. 7 ff.

[2] *Deutsche Kolonialreform*, pp. 1396-1397. One must not forget that the book was written in 1905. Since then the interrelation of forces, and the map of the world, have undergone material changes.

spreading of the organisational forms of modern capital, capital export is nothing but a seizure and a monopolisation of new spheres of capital investment by the monopoly enterprises of a great nation or—taking the process as a whole—by the organised "national" industry, by "national" finance capital. Capital export is the most convenient method for the economic policy of finance groups; it subjugates new territories with the greatest ease. This is why the sharpening of competition between various states is most salient here. The internationalisation of economic life here, too, makes it necessary to settle controversial questions by fire and sword.

CHAPTER VIII

World Economy and the "National" State

1. REPRODUCTION OF WORLD CAPITAL AND THE ROOTS OF CAPI-
TALIST EXPANSION. 2. OVERPRODUCTION OF INDUSTRIAL GOODS,
UNDERPRODUCTION OF AGRICULTURAL PRODUCTS, AND OVERPRODUC-
TION OF CAPITAL AS THREE FACETS OF THE SAME PHENOMENON. 3.
CONFLICT BETWEEN WORLD ECONOMY AND THE LIMITATIONS OF THE
"NATIONAL" STATE. 4. IMPERIALISM AS THE POLICY OF FINANCE
CAPITAL. 5. IDEOLOGY OF IMPERIALISM.

FROM the point of view of the ruling circles of society, frictions and conflicts between "national" groups of the bourgeoisie,
inevitably arising inside of present-day society, lead in their
further development to war as the only solution of the problem.
We have seen that those frictions and conflicts are caused by
the changes that have taken place in the conditions of reproducing world capital. Capitalist society, built on a number of
antagonistic elements, can maintain a relative equilibrium only
at the price of painful crises; the adaptation of the various
parts of the social organism to each other and to the whole
can be achieved only with a colossal waste of energy, under
tremendous *"faux frais"* of this adaptation, which flow from
the character of capitalist society as such, *i.e.*, from a definite
historical formulation of the development in general.

We have laid bare three fundamental motives for the conquest policies of modern capitalist states: increased competition
in the sales markets, in the markets of raw materials, and for
the spheres of capital investment. This is what the modern
development of capitalism and its transformation into finance
capitalism has brought about.

Those three roots of the policy of finance capitalism, however, represent in substance only three facets of the same
phenomenon, namely of the conflict between the growth of
productive forces on the one hand, and the "national" limits
of the production organisation on the other.

Indeed, overproduction of manufactured goods is at the same time underproduction of agricultural products. Underproduction of agricultural products is in this case important for us in so far as the demand on the part of industry is excessively large, *i.e.*, in so far as there are large volumes of manufactured goods which cannot be exchanged for agricultural products; in so far as the ratio between those two branches of production has been (and is more and more) disturbed. This is why growing industry seeks for an agrarian "economic supplement" which, within the framework of capitalism, particularly its monopoly form, *i.e.*, finance capital, inevitably expresses itself in the form of subjugating agrarian countries by force of arms.

We have just discussed the exchange of commodities. Capital export, however, does not represent an isolated phenomenon, either. Capital export, as we have seen, is due to a certain overproduction of capital. Overproduction of capital, however, is nothing but another formulation for overproduction of commodities:

> Overproduction of capital [says Marx] never signifies anything else but overproduction of means of production—means of production and necessities of life—which may serve as capital, that is, serve for the exploitation of labour at a given degree of exploitation. . . . Capital consists of commodities, and therefore the overproduction of capital implies an overproduction of commodities.[1]

Conversely, when the overproduction of capital decreases, there is also a decrease in the overproduction of commodities. This is why capital export, in decreasing overproduction of capital, aids also in decreasing the overproduction of commodities. (Let us note parenthetically that if, for instance, iron beams are exported into another country to be sold there, we have commodity export pure and simple; if, however, the beam-producing firm establishes an enterprise in another country and exports its commodities to equip the enterprise, we have capital export; obviously, the criterion is whether the transactions of purchase and sale take place or not.)

But even aside from simply "relieving the congestion" by exporting capital in commodity form, there is also a further connection between capital export and the decrease in the over-

[1] *Capital*, Vol. III, pp. 300-301.

production of commodities. Otto Bauer has very well formulated this connection.

Thus [he says] the exploitation of economically backward countries by the capitalists of a European country has two series of consequences: directly, it creates new spheres of investment for capital in the colonial country, and at the same time more selling opportunities for the industry of the dominating power; indirectly, it creates new spheres for the application of capital also inside of the dominating country, and increases the sale of the products of all its industries.[1]

If we thus consider the problem in its entirety, and take thereby the objective point of view, *i.e.*, the point of view of the adaptation of modern society to its conditions of existence, we find that there is here a growing discord between the basis of social economy which has become world-wide and the peculiar class structure of society, a structure where the ruling class (the bourgeoisie) itself is split into "national" groups with contradictory economic interests, groups which, being opposed to the world proletariat, are competing among themselves for the division of the surplus value created on a world scale. Production is of a social nature; international division of labour turns the private "national" economies into parts of a gigantic all-embracing labour process, which extends over almost the whole of humanity. Acquisition, however, assumes the character of "national" (state) acquisition where the beneficiaries are huge state companies of the bourgeoisie of finance capital. The development of productive forces moves within the narrow limits of state boundaries while it has already outgrown those limits. Under such conditions there inevitably arises a conflict, which, given the existence of capitalism, is settled through extending the state frontiers in bloody struggles, a settlement which holds the prospect of new and more grandiose conflicts.

The social representatives of this contradiction are the various groups of the bourgeoisie organised in the state, with their conflicting interests. The development of world capitalism leads, on the one hand, to an internationalisation of the eco-

[1] Otto Bauer: *Die Nationalitätenfrage und die Sozialdemokratie*, Vienna, 1907, p. 464.

nomic life and, on the other, to the leveling of economic differences,—and to an infinitely greater degree, the same process of economic development intensifies the tendency to "nationalise" capitalist interests, to form narrow "national" groups armed to the teeth and ready to hurl themselves at one another any moment. It is impossible to describe the fundamental aims of present-day politics better than was done by R. Hilferding. "The policy of finance capital," he says, "pursues a threefold aim: first, the creation of the largest possible economic territory which, secondly, must be protected against foreign competition by tariff walls, and thus, thirdly, must become an area of exploitation for the national monopoly companies." [1] The increase in the economic territory opens agrarian regions to the national cartels and, consequently, markets for raw materials, increasing the sales markets and the sphere of capital investment; the tariff policy makes it possible to suppress foreign competition, to obtain surplus profit, and to put into operation the battering ram of dumping; the "system" as a whole facilitates the increase of the rate of profit for the monopoly organisations. This policy of finance capital is imperialism.

Such a policy implies violent methods, for the expansion of the state territory means war. The reverse, however, is not true; not every war or every increase in the state territory implies an imperialist policy. The determining factor is whether the war expresses the policy of finance capital, the latter term being taken in accordance with the above definition. Here, as everywhere, we find some intermediary forms, whose existence, however, by no means vitiates the main definition. This is why attempts like those made by the well-known Italian economist and sociologist, Achille Loria, are fundamentally incorrect. Loria, namely, has attempted to construct two conceptions of imperialism which, he alleges, contain "entirely heterogeneous relations" (*des rélations tout à fait hétérogènes*). Loria distinguishes [2] between "economic" imperialism (*l'impérialisme économique, ökonomischer Imperialismus*) and "commercial" or "trade" imperialism (*l'impérial-*

---

[1] Rudolf Hilferding: *Finanzkapital*, p. 412.
[2] Achille Loria, "Les deux notions de l'impérialisme," in *Revue économique internationale*, 1907, Vol. 3, p. 459 *ff*.

isme commercial, Handelsimperialismus). The object of the former, he says, are tropical countries, the object of the latter are countries whose conditions make them suitable also for European colonisation; the method of the former is armed force, the method of the latter, peaceful treaties (*des accords pacifiques*); the former has no shadings or grades, in the latter they range from the maximum of full assimilation or a single tariff to incomplete forms, like preference tariffs between the colonies and the mother countries, etc.

This is Loria's theory. It is quite obvious that it is made out of whole cloth. Both the "commercial" and the "economic" imperialisms are in substance the expression of the same tendencies, as we have seen above. A closed ring of tariff duties, and the raising of the latter, may not result in an armed conflict immediately; they will, however, bring about such a conflict later. It is thus obvious that we cannot contrast "peaceful treaties" with "armed forces." (Peaceful treaties between England and its colonies mean a straining of the relations between England and other countries.) Neither can we assert that "economic" imperialism is merely of a "tropical" nature. The best proof is the fate of Belgium, Galicia, and the probable fate of South America, China, Turkey, and Persia.

To sum up: the development of the productive forces of world capitalism has made gigantic strides in the last decades. The upper hand in the competitive struggle has everywhere been gained by large-scale production; it has consolidated the "magnates of capital" into an ironclad organisation, which has taken possession of the entire economic life. State power has become the domain of a financial oligarchy; the latter manages production which is tied up by the banks into one knot. This process of the organisation of production has proceeded from below; it has fortified itself within the framework of modern states, which have become an exact expression of the interests of finance capital. Every one of the capitalistically advanced "national economies" has turned into some kind of a "national" trust. This process of the organisation of the economically advanced sections of world economy, on the other hand, has been accompanied by an extraordinary sharpening of their mutual competition. The overproduction of

. . .

commodities, which is connected with the growth of large enter-prises; the export policy of the cartels, and the narrowing of the sales markets in connection with the colonial and tariff policy of the capitalist powers; the growing disproportion be-tween tremendously developed industry and backward agricul-ture; the gigantic growth of capital export and the economic subjugation of entire regions by "national" banking combines— all this has thrown into the sharpest possible relief the clash of interests between the "national" groups of capital. Those groups find their final argument in the force and power of the state organisation, first of all in its army and navy. A mighty state military power is the last trump in the struggle of the powers. The fighting force in the world market thus depends upon the power and consolidation of the "nation," upon its financial and military resources. A self-sufficient national state, and an economic unit limitlessly expending its great power until it becomes a world kingdom—a world-wide empire —such is the ideal built up by finance capital.

With a steady and clear eye does it [finance capital] view the Babylonian confusion of peoples, and above all of them it sees its own nation. The latter is real; it lives in a powerful state, which keeps on increasing its power and grandeur, and which devotes all its forces to making them greater. In this way, the interests of the individual are subjugated to the interests of the whole—a condition without which no social ideology can live; a nation and a state that are hostile to the people are tied into one whole, and the national idea, as a motive power, is subjugated to politics. The class con-flicts have disappeared; they have been annihilated, absorbed as they are in serving the interests of the whole. In place of the dangerous class struggle, fraught for the owners with unknown consequences, there appear the general actions of the nation which is united by one aim—the striving for national grandeur.[1]

Thus the interests of finance capital acquire a grandiose ideological formulation; every effort is made to inculcate it into the mass of workers, for, as a German imperialist has correctly remarked from his point of view: "We must gain power not only over the legs of the soldiers, but also over their minds and hearts." [2]

[1] Rudolf Hilferding, *l.c.*, pp. 428-429.
[2] *Die deutsche Finanz-Reform der Zukunft,* part III of the book *Staatsstreich oder Reformen* by Ein Ausland-Deutscher, Zurich, 1907, p. 203.

PART III

IMPERIALISM AS THE REPRODUCTION OF CAPITALIST COMPETITION ON A LARGER SCALE

CHAPTER IX

Imperialism as an Historic Category

1. THE VULGAR UNDERSTANDING OF IMPERIALISM. 2. ROLE OF POLITICS IN SOCIAL LIFE. 3. METHODOLOGY OF CLASSIFICATION IN SOCIAL SCIENCES. 4. EPOCH OF FINANCE CAPITAL AS HISTORIC CATEGORY. 5. IMPERIALISM AS HISTORIC CATEGORY.

IN the preceding chapters we undertook to prove that imperialist policies arise only on a certain level of historic development. A number of contradictions of capitalism are here tied up into one knot, which is cut by the sword of war, only to be tied again more tightly the next moment. The policy of the ruling classes, and their ideology inevitably arising from this stage of development, must therefore be characterised as a specific phenomenon.[1]

In the literature that floods the market at present, there prevail two, *soi-disant*, theories of imperialism. One sees in the modern policy of conquest a struggle of races. The "Slavs" or the "Teutonic" races are supposed to strive for domination, and all virtues and vices are distributed among those "races" according to the nationality of the author. Old and vulgar as this "theory" is, it persists with a tenacity of a prejudice, for it finds a very favourable soil in the growth of "national self-consciousness" among the ruling classes who are directly interested in utilising the remnants of old psychological strati-

[1] We speak of imperialism mainly as of a *policy* of finance capital. However, one may also speak of imperialism as an *ideology*. In a similar way *liberalism* is on the one hand a policy of industrial capitalism (free trade, etc.), on the other hand it denotes a whole ideology (personal liberty, etc.).

fications for the interest of the state organisation of finance capital.

A simple reference to facts shatters this theory, leaving not a single stone of the entire edifice. The Anglo-Saxons, of the same origin as the Germans, are their cruelest enemies; the Bulgarians and the Serbs, pure Slavs, speaking almost the same language, find themselves on different sides of the trenches. The Poles are recruiting among themselves ardent partisans of both Austrian and Russian orientation. The same is happening with the Ukrainians, one section of whom is in sympathy with the Russians, while another is in sympathy with the Austrians. On the other hand, every one of the belligerent coalitions combines the most heterogeneous races, nationalities, tribes. Looked at from a racial point of view, what is there common to the English, Italians, Russians, Spanish and the black savages of the French colonies, whom the "glorious republic" is driving to slaughter, just as the ancient Romans drove their colonial slaves? What is there common to the Germans and the Czechs, the Ukrainians and the Hungarians, the Bulgarians and the Turks who proceed together against the coalition of the Entente? It is perfectly obvious that not races but state organisations of definite groups of the bourgeoisie are conducting the struggle. It is also perfectly obvious that one or the other grouping of the great powers is determined, not by a community of certain racial tasks, but by a community of capitalist aims at a given moment. This is why the Serbs and Bulgarians, who only recently fought together against Turkey, have now split into hostile camps. This is why England, formerly an enemy of Russia, is now exercising hegemony over it. This is why Japan keeps step with the Russian bourgeoisie, although only ten years ago Japanese capital fought with arms in hand against Russian capital.[1]

From a purely scientific, not falsified, point of view, the inadequacy of this theory is striking. Notwithstanding its obvious falsity, however, it is assiduously cultivated both in the press and in the universities, for the sole reason that it

[1] The "racial theory" has been excellently ridiculed by Kautsky. See his: *Rasse und Judentum*, published during the war. [Published in English under the title *Are the Jews a Race*, 1926.—Ed.]

promises no mean advantages for Master Capital.[1] In justice, however, we must note that, to the extent that the various "races" are being consolidated and united in the iron fist of the military state, there appears a less vulgar but no less untenable attempt to advance a territorial-psychological theory. The place of the "race" is here taken by its substitute, the "middle European," "American," or some other "humanity."[2] This theory is also far from the truth, because it ignores the principal characteristic of modern society—its class structure, and because the class interests of the upper social strata are substituted for the so-called "general" interests of the "whole."

The second very widespread "theory" of imperialism defines it as the policy of conquest in general. From this point of view one can speak with equal right of Alexander the Macedonian's and the Spanish conquerors' imperialism, of the imperialism of Carthage and Ivan III, of ancient Rome and modern America, of Napoleon and Hindenburg.

Simple as this theory may be, it is absolutely untrue. It is untrue because it "explains" everything, *i.e.*, it explains absolutely nothing.

Every policy of the ruling classes ("pure" policy, military policy, economic policy) has a perfectly definite functional significance. Growing out of the soil of a given system of production, it serves to reproduce given relations of production either simply or on an enlarged scale. The policy of the feudal rulers strengthens and widens feudal production relations. The policy of trade capital increases the sphere of domination of trade capitalism. The policy of finance capitalism reproduces the production basis of finance capital on a wider scale.

It is perfectly clear that the same thing can also be said about the war. War serves to reproduce definite relations of production. War of conquest serves to reproduce those rela-

---

[1] "Scientific" literature of the war period abounds with monstrous examples of barbarous violations of the most elementary truths. All possible methods are being picked up to show the cultural bankruptcy and the inborn meanness of the enemy's "race" (*minderwertige Nationen*). A French magazine has published a so-called "investigation" earnestly proving to its readers that the German urine is one-third more poisonous than that of the Entente nations in general, that of the French in particular!

[2] See F. Neumann: *Mitteleuropa.*

tions on a wider scale. Simply to define war, however, as conquest is entirely insufficient, for the simple reason that in doing so we fail to indicate the main thing, namely, *what* production relations are strengthened or extended by the war, what basis is widened by a given "policy of conquest." [1]

Bourgeois science does not see and does not wish to see this. It does not understand that a basis for the classification of various "policies" must exist in the social economy out of which the "policies" arise. Moreover, it is inclined to overlook the vast differences existing between various periods of economic development, and just at the present time, when all the peculiarities of the historical economic process of our days are so striking to the eye, the Austrian and Anglo-American economic school, the least historical of all, has built its nest in bourgeois economics.[2] Publicists and scholars attempt to paint modern imperialism as something akin to the policies of the heroes of antiquity with their "imperium."

This is the "method" of bourgeois historians and economists. They gloss over the fundamental difference between the slaveholding system of "antiquity," with its embryo of trade capital and artisanship, and "modern capitalism." The aim in this case is quite clear. The futility of the ideas of labour democracy must be "proven" by placing it on a level with the *Lumpenproletariat*, the workers and the artisans of antiquity.

From a purely scientific point of view all such theories are highly erroneous. If a certain phase of development is to be theoretically understood, it must be understood with all its peculiarities, its distinguishing trends, its specific characteristics, which it shares with none. He who, like "Colonel Torrence," sees in the savage's club the beginning of capital, he who, like the "Austrian" school of economics, defines capital as a means of production (which in essence is the same thing), will never be able to find his way among the tendencies of

---

[1] Clausewitz's declaration that war is a continuation of politics by other means, is well known. Politics itself, however, is an active "continuation" in space of a given mode of production.

[2] It is curious to note that even such scientists as the Russian historian, R. Wipper, have an unusual liking for "modernising" events beyond all bounds, for obliterating all historical marks. This is no surprise, for in very recent times Wipper has revealed himself as an unbridled chauvinist calumniator, finding hospitality at Mr. Riabushinsky's [Riabushinsky was a prominent Russian manufacturer.—*Ed.*]

capitalist development and include them in one theoretical structure. The historian or economist who places under one denominator the structure of modern capitalism, *i.e.*, modern production relations, and the numerous types of production relations that formerly led to wars of conquest, will understand nothing in the development of modern world economy. One must single out the specific elements which characterise our time, and analyse them. This was *Marx's* method, and this is how a Marxist must approach the analysis of imperialism.[1]

/ We now understand that it is impossible to confine oneself to the analysis of the forms, in which a policy manifests itself; for instance, one cannot be satisfied with defining a policy as that of "conquest," "expansion," "violence," etc. One must analyse the basis on which it rises and which it serves to widen. We have defined imperialism as the policy of finance capital. Therewith we uncovered the functional significance of that policy. It upholds the structure of finance capital; it subjugates the world to the domination of finance capital; in place of the old pre-capitalist, or the old capitalist, production relations, it put the production relations of finance capital. Just as finance capitalism (which must not be confused with money capital, for finance capital is characterised by being simultaneously banking *and* industrial capital) is an historically limited epoch, confined only to the last few decades, so imperialism, as the policy of finance capital, is a specific historic category.

Imperialism is a policy of conquest. But not every policy of conquest is imperialism. Finance capital cannot pursue any other policy. This is why, when we speak of imperialism as the policy of finance capital, its conquest character is self-understood; at the same time, however, we point out what production relations are being reproduced by this policy of conquest. Moreover, this definition also includes a whole series of other historic trends and characteristics. Indeed, when we speak of finance capital, we imply highly developed economic organisms and, consequently, a certain scope and intensity of

[1] The methodology of Marxian economics was brilliantly explained by Marx in his *Einleitung zu einer Kritik der politischen Oekonomie*, which was published by Kautsky as an appendix to the latest edition of *Zur Kritik der politischen Oekonomie*, Stuttgart, 1897. [In English translation: *A Contribution to the Critique of Political Economy*, Chicago, 1913.—*Ed.*]

world relations; in a word, we imply the existence of a developed world economy; by the same token we imply a certain state of production relations, of organisational forms of the economic life, a certain interrelation of classes, and also a certain *future* of economic relations, etc., etc. Even the form and the means of struggle, the organisation of state power, the military technique, etc., are taken to be a more or less definite entity, whereas the formula "policy of conquest" is good for pirates, for caravan trade, and also for imperialism. In other words, the formula "policy of conquest," defines nothing, whereas the formula, "policy of conquest of finance capital," characterises imperialism as a definite historical entity.

From the fact that the epoch of finance capitalism is an historically limited phenomenon, it does not follow, of course, that it has stepped into the light of day like *Deus ex machina*. In reality it is an historic continuation of the epoch of industrial capitalism, just as the latter was a continuation of the phase of commercial capitalism. This is why the fundamental contradictions of capitalism which, in the course of its development, are continually being reproduced on a wider scale, find their sharpest expression in our own epoch. The same is true of the anarchic structure of capitalism, which finds its expression in competition. The anarchic character of capitalist society is expressed in the fact that social economy is not an organised collective body guided by a single will, but a system of economies interconnected through exchange, each of which produces at its own risk, never being in a position to adapt itself more or less to the volume of social demand and to the production carried on in other individual economies. This calls forth a struggle of the economies against each other, a war of capitalist competition. The forms of this competition can be widely different. The imperialist policy in particular is one of the forms of the competitive struggle. In the following chapter we intend to analyse it as a case of capitalist competition, namely, competition in the epoch of finance capital.

CHAPTER X

Reproduction of the Processes of Concentration and Centralisation of Capital on a World Scale

1. CONCENTRATION OF CAPITAL. CONCENTRATION OF CAPITAL IN SINGLE ENTERPRISES. CONCENTRATION OF CAPITAL IN TRUSTS. CONCENTRATION OF CAPITAL IN ORGANISED "NATIONAL ECONOMIES" ("STATE CAPITALIST TRUSTS"). 2. CENTRALISATION OF CAPITAL. 3. STRUGGLE BETWEEN INDIVIDUAL ENTERPRISES; STRUGGLE BETWEEN TRUSTS; STRUGGLE BETWEEN "STATE CAPITALIST TRUSTS." 4. PRESENT-DAY CAPITALIST EXPANSION AS A CASE OF CAPITAL CENTRALISATION. ABSORPTION OF SIMILAR STRUCTURES (HORIZONTAL CENTRALISATION). ABSORPTION OF AGRARIAN REGIONS (VERTICAL CENTRALISATION. COMBINE).

THE two most important processes of capitalist development are concentration and centralisation of capital; they are often confused but must be clearly distinguished. This is how Marx defines these terms:

Every individual capital [he says] is a larger or smaller concentration of the means of production, giving command over a larger or smaller army of workers. Every accumulation becomes the means of new accumulation. As the mass of wealth which functions as capital increases, there goes on an increasing concentration of that wealth in the hands of individual capitalists, with a resultant widening of the basis of large-scale production and of the specific methods of capitalist production. The growth of social capital is affected by the growth of many individual capitals. . . . Two points characterise this kind of concentration *which is directly dependant upon accumulation, or, rather, identical with it* [*italics ours—N.B.*]. First of all, the increasing concentration of the social means of production into the hands of individual capitals, is, other conditions being equal, restricted by the extent of social wealth. In the second place, the part of social capital domiciled in each particular sphere of production is divided among many capitalists, who face one another as independent commodity producers competing one with another. . . . This splitting up of social capital into a number of individual capitals, or the repulsion of its fragments one by another, [Marx here has in mind the division of property, etc.—*N.B.*], is counteracted by their attraction. The latter is not simply a concentration of the means of production and command over labour identical with accumulation. It is the concentration of already formed capitals, the destruction of their individual independence, the expropriation of capitalist by capitalist, the transformation of many small capitals into a few large ones. This process is distinguished from simple accumulation by this, that it involves nothing more than a change in the distribution of capitals that already exist and are already at work. . . . Capital aggregates into great masses in one hand because, elsewhere, it is taken out of my hands. Here we have genuine centralisation in contradistinction to accumulation and concentration.[1]

To summarise. By concentration we understand the increase of capital that is due to the capitalisation of the surplus value produced by that capital; under centralisation we understand the joining together of various individual capital units which thus form a new larger unit. Concentration and centralisation of capital pass through various phases of development, which we must now survey. Let us note in passing that both processes, concentration and centralisation, influence one another. A great concentration of capital accelerates the absorption of small-scale enterprises by large-scale ones; conversely, centralisation aids the increase of individual capital units and so accelerates the process of concentration.

The primary form in the process of concentration is concentration of capital in an individual enterprise. This form predominated up to the last quarter of the nineteenth century. The accumulation of social capital is here expressed in the accumulation of the capital of individual entrepreneurs who oppose one another as competitors. The development of joint stock companies, which made it possible to use the capital of a considerable number of individual entrepreneurs, and which radically undermined the principle of individual ownership of enterprises, created the prerequisites for large monopolistic associations of entrepreneurs. Concentration of capital assumed a new form here, namely, the form of *concentration in trusts.* Capital accumulation no more increased the capital of individual producers; it turned into a means of increasing the capi-

[1] *Capital,* Vol. I, pp. 690-691.

tal of entrepreneurs' organisations. The tempo of accumulation increased to an extraordinary degree. Huge masses of surplus value, far exceeding the needs of an insignificant group of capitalists, are converted into capital to begin a new cycle. But even here the development does not stop. The individual production branches are in various ways knit together into one collective body, organised on a large scale. Finance capital seizes the entire country in an iron grip. "National economy" turns into one gigantic combined trust whose partners are the financial groups and the state. Such formations we call state capitalist trusts. Of course, the latter formations cannot be identified with the structure of a trust in the proper sense of the word; a trust proper is a much more centralised and less anarchic organisation. To a certain degree, however, particularly in comparison with the preceding phase of capitalism, the economically developed states have already advanced far towards a situation where they can be looked upon as big trust-like organisations or, as we have termed them, state capitalist trusts. We may, therefore, speak at present about the concentration of capital in state capitalist trusts as component parts of a much larger socio-economic entity, world economy.

It is true that the early economists already spoke of the "accumulation of capital in a country," this being one of the favourite subjects, as witnessed, for instance, by the title of Adam Smith's principal book. At that time, however, the expression had a considerably different meaning, for "national economy," or the "economy of a country" by no means represented a collective capitalist enterprise, a single gigantic combined trust—a form largely adopted at present by the foremost capitalist countries.

Parallel with the change in the forms of concentration went the change in the forms of centralisation. Where individual ownership of enterprises prevailed, individual capitalists opposed one another in the competitive struggle. At that time "national economy" and "world economy" were only sum totals of those comparatively small units that were interconnected by the circulation of commodities and competed with each other mainly within "national" limits. The centralisation process consisted in small capitalists being absorbed by large ones, in the growth of large-scale, individually owned, enterprises. With the growth of large-scale enterprises the extensive character of competition (within given territorial limits) decreased more and more; the number of competitors shrank with the growth of centralisation. On the other hand, the intensity of the competition increased tremendously, for the smaller number of larger enterprises began to place on the market volumes of commodities unknown in former times. Concentration and centralisation of capital finally brought about the formation of trusts. Competition rose to a still higher stage. Where formerly many individually owned enterprises competed with one another, there appeared the most stubborn competition between a few gigantic capitalist combines pursuing a complicated and, to a considerable degree, calculated policy. There finally comes a time when competition ceases in an entire branch of production. But the war for dividing up the surplus value between the syndicates of the various branches becomes fiercer; organisations producing manufactured goods arise against syndicates producing raw materials, and vice versa. The centralisation process proceeds apace. Combines in industry and banking syndicates unite the entire "national" production, which assumes the form of a company of companies, thus becoming a state capitalist trust. Competition reaches the highest, the last conceivable state of development. It is now the competition of state capitalist trusts in the world market. Competition is reduced to a minimum within the boundaries of "national" economies, only to flare up in colossal proportions, such as would not have been possible in any of the preceding historic epochs. Of course, there existed competition between "national economies," i.e., between their ruling classes, also in former times. That competition, however, was of an entirely different nature, for the inner structure of those "national economies" was entirely different. "National economy" did not appear on the arena of the world market as a homogeneous organised whole endowed with unusual economic strength; inside of it absolutely free competition reigned. On the other hand, competition in the world market was extremely weak. All this looks entirely different now in the epoch of finance capitalism, when the centre of gravity is shifted to the competition of gigantic, consolidated, and organised economic bodies possessed of a colossal fighting capacity in the world tournament of "nations." Here competition holds its orgies on the greatest possible scale, and together with this there goes on a change and a shift to a higher phase in the process of capital centralisation. The absorption of small capital units by large ones, the absorption of weak trusts, the absorption even of large trusts by larger ones is relegated to the rear, and looks like child's play compared with the absorption of whole countries that are being forcibly torn away from their economic centres and included in the economic system of the victorious "nation." Imperialist annexation is only a case of the general capitalist tendency towards centralisation of capital, a case of its centralisation on that maximum scale which corresponds to the competition of state capitalist trusts. The arena of this combat is world economy; its economic and political limits are a world trust, a single world state obedient to the finance capital of the victors who assimilate all the rest—an ideal of which even the hottest heads of former epochs never dreamed.

One may distinguish two kinds of centralisation: the one where an economic unit absorbs another unit of the same kind, and the one which we term vertical centralisation, where an economic unit absorbs another of a different kind. In the latter case we have "economic supplement" or combination. At present, when the competition and the centralisation of capital are being reproduced on a world scale, we find the same two types. When one country, one state capitalist trust, absorbs another, a weaker one possessed of comparatively the same economic structure, we have a horizontal centralisation of capital. Where, however, the state capitalist trust includes an economically supplementary unit, an agrarian country for instance, we have the formation of a combine. Substantially the same contradictions and the same moving forces are reflected here as within the limits of "national economies"; to be specific, the rise of prices of raw materials leads to the rise of combined enterprises. Thus on the higher stage of the struggle there is reproduced the same contradiction between the various branches, but on a considerably wider scale.

The actual process of development of modern world economy knows both these forms. An example of a horizontal imperialist annexation is the seizure of Belgium by Germany; an example of vertical annexation is the seizure of Egypt by England. None the less, it is customary to reduce imperialism to colonial conquests alone. This entirely erroneous conception formerly found some justification in the fact that the bourgeoisie, following the line of least resistance, tended to widen its territory by the seizure of free lands that offered little resistance. Now, however, the time has come for a fundamental redivision. Just as trusts competing with one another within the boundaries of a state first grow at the expense of "third persons," of outsiders, and only after having destroyed the intermediary groupings, thrust themselves against one another with particular ferocity, so the competitive struggle between state capitalist trusts first expresses itself in a struggle for free lands, for the *jus primi occupantis,* then it stages a redivision of colonies, and finally, when the struggle becomes more intense, even the territory of the home country is drawn into the process of redivision. Here, too, development proceeds along the line of least resistance, and the weakest state capitalist trusts first disappear from the face of the earth. This is the general law of capitalist production, which can fall only with the fall of capitalist production itself.

CHAPTER XI

Means of Competitive Struggle, and State Power

1. Means of struggle between individually owned enterprises. 2. Means of struggle between trusts. 3. Means of struggle between state capitalist trusts. 4. Economic significance of state power. 5. Militarism. 6. Change in the structure of state power.

The growth of competition outlined in the last chapter reduces itself to the fact that the continuous elimination of competition among smaller economic units calls forth a sharper competition among large economic units. This process is accompanied by curious changes in the methods of struggle.

The struggle of individually owned enterprises is usually conducted by means of low prices; small shops sell cheaper, reducing their standards of living to a minimum; capitalists strive to reduce the production costs by improving technique and lowering wages, etc. When the struggle among individually owned enterprises has been replaced by the struggle among trusts, the methods of struggle (in so far as it is conducted in the world market) undergo a certain change; low prices disappear in the home market, being replaced by high prices which facilitate the struggle in the world market; the latter is conducted by means of low prices at the expense of the high prices paid in the home market. The importance of state power grows: tariff rates, freight rates are taken advantage of; the tremendous economic power of the trusts opposing one another, both in the domestic and in the foreign market, allows them, under certain conditions, also to apply other methods. When a trust represents a large combined enterprise, when, for instance, it owns railroads, steamboats, electric power, etc., thus forming a state within a state, it can pursue a very complicated policy in regard to its competitors by regulating railroad rates, water transport rates, by establishing prices for the use of electric power, etc., etc. Of still

122

greater significance is the closing of an access to raw materials and to the sales market, as well as the refusal of credit. The road to raw materials is usually blocked where there is a combined cartel. Raw materials produced by enterprises belonging to the cartel are not sold to outsiders "as a matter of principle" (the so-called *ausschliesslicher Verbandsverkehr*); as to the sales markets, here the organisations belonging to the cartel agree to buy nothing from outsiders; moreover, this, under the pressure of the cartel, is made binding also for "third persons" who usually buy from the cartel (for which they sometimes receive premiums, reductions, etc.). We must finally note a lowering of prices and selling at a loss to stifle the competitor. The trust here declares that "it does not wish to make profit on the enterprise itself, that the struggle is conducted only to defeat the competitor, and therefore without any relation to self-cost. The lower limit is formed, not by the production costs, but by the cartel's capital power and by the strength of its credit; the question thus reduces itself to how long its members will be able to stand a struggle which, for the time being, offers them no gain."[1] In the home market this method is used to stamp out the final resistance of the opponent; in the foreign market it appears only as an increase of dumping. There are, however, still more striking examples of the struggle. We have in mind the struggle among the American trusts. The principles applied here went far beyond what is permissible in organised government: criminal gangs were hired to destroy railroad tracks, to damage and blow up oil pipes; incendiarism and murder were practiced; governmental authorities, including entire judicial bodies, were bribed on a large scale; spies were maintained in the camp of the competitors, etc., etc.—there is a plethora of material in this respect in the history of the giant American combines.[2]

When competition has finally reached its highest stage, when it has become competition between state capitalist trusts, then

---

[1] Fritz Kestner: *Der Organisationszwang. Eine Untersuchung über die Kämpfe zwischen den Kartellen und Aussenseitern*, Berlin, 1912. Commenting on Kestner is Hilferding's article, "Organisationsmacht und Staatsgewalt," in the *Neue Zeit*, 32, 2.

[2] *Cf.* Gustavus Myers: *History of the Great American Fortunes*, Chicago, 1909.

the use of state power, and the possibilities connected with it, begin to play a very large part. The state apparatus has always served as a tool in the hands of the ruling classes of its country, and it has always acted as their "defender and protector" in the world market; at no time, however, did it have the colossal importance that it has in the epoch of finance capital and imperialist politics. With the formation of state capitalist trusts, competition is being almost entirely shifted to foreign countries; obviously, the organs of the struggle that is to be waged abroad, primarily state power, must therefore grow tremendously. The significance for capitalism of high tariffs, which increase the fighting capacity of the state capitalist trust in the world market, must increase still more; the various forms of "protecting national industry" become more pronounced; state orders are placed only with "national" firms; income is guaranteed to all sorts of enterprises, which present great risks but are "useful" from a social point of view; the activities of "foreigners" are hampered in various ways. (Compare, for instance, the stock exchange policy of the French government as mentioned in Chapter II). Whenever a question arises about changing commercial treaties, the state power of the contracting groups of capitalists appears on the scene, and the mutual relations of those states—reduced in the final analysis to the relations between their military forces—determine the treaty. When a loan is to be granted to one or the other country, the government, basing itself on military power, secures the highest possible rate of interest for its nationals, guarantees obligatory orders, stipulates concessions, struggles against foreign competitors. When the struggle begins for the exploitation by finance capital of a territory that has not been formally occupied by anybody, again the military power of the state decides who will possess that territory. In "peaceful" times the military state apparatus is hidden behind the scenes where it never stops functioning; in war times it appears on the scene most directly. The more strained the situation in the world sphere of struggle—and our epoch is characterised by the greatest intensity of competition between "national" groups of finance capital—the oftener an appeal is made to the mailed fist of state power.

The remnants of the old *laissez faire, laissez passer* ideology disappear, the epoch of the new "mercantilism," of imperialism, begins.

The tendency towards imperialism combines economic phenomena with a great political power. Everything is organised on a large scale. The free play of economic forces, not so long ago highly alluring to thinkers and men of affairs, dies out. There is an ebb and flow of migrating people everywhere, and that process is supervised by the state. The new economic and social forces require powerful protection both inside the country and outside of its frontiers; for this purpose the state creates new organs, great numbers of officials and institutions. State activities are everywhere enlarged by new functions. Its influence over the facts of home life and over foreign relations becomes more multifarious. The government would not decline directly to look after the interests of its people [the term "people" must, of course, be understood conditionally when reading bourgeois economists—*N.B.*] at whatever point of the globe the interests may appear. National economy and politics are most closely interlocked. The breach between this epoch and the epoch of old liberalism, with its advocacy of free play, with its doctrine of the harmony of interests, becomes ever wider. This makes one think that there is more cruelty and pugnacity in the world as a whole. The world is more united than ever: everything is contiguous to everything, everything is influenced by everything, at the same time everybody jostles against everybody else, and deals blows right and left.[1]

If state power is generally growing in significance, the growth of its military organisation, the army and the navy, is particularly striking. The struggle between state capitalist trusts is decided in the first place by the relation between their military forces, for the military power of the country is the last resort of the struggling "national" groups of capitalists. The immensely growing state budget devotes an ever larger share to "defence purposes," as militarisation is euphemistically termed.

The following table illustrates the monstrous growth of military expenditures and their share in the state budget.

[1] Prof. Isayev, *l.c.*, pp. 261-262.

COST OF ARMY AND NAVY

States	Years	Military expenditures per capita of the population	All state expenditures per capita of the population	Percentage of military expenditures in relation to all expenditures	Years	Military expenditures per capita of the population	All state expenditures per capita of the population	Percentage of military expenditures in relation to all expenditures
England	1875	16.10	41.67	38.06	1907-08	26.42	54.83	48.6
France	1875	15.23	52.71	29.0	1908	24.81	67.04	37.0
Austria-Hungary	1873	5.92	22.05	26.8	1908	8.49	37.01	22.8
Italy	1874	6.02	31.44	19.1	1907-08	9.53	33.24	28.7
Russia	1877	5.24	15.14	34.6	1908	7.42	20.81	35.6
Japan	1875	0.60	3.48	17.2	1908	4.53	18.08	25.1
Germany	1881-82	9.43	33.07	28.5	1908	18.44	65.22	28.3
United States of America	1875	10.02	29.89	33.5	1907-08	16.68	29.32	56.9 1

The present military budgets are expressed in the following figures: the United States (1914), $173,522,804 for the army and $139,682,186 for the navy, total $313,204,990; France (1913), 983,224,376 francs for the army and 467,176,109 francs for the navy, total 1,450,400,485 francs (in 1914, 1,717,202,233 francs); Russia (1913, counting only ordinary expenditures), 581,099,921 rubles for the army and 244,846,-500 rubles for the navy, total 825,946,421 rubles; Great Britain (1913-14), 28,220,000 pounds for the army and 48,-809,300 pounds for the navy, total 77,029,300 pounds; Germany (1913, both ordinary and extraordinary expenditure), 97,845,960 pounds sterling, etc.[2]

We are now passing through a period when armaments on land, on water, and in the air are growing with feverish rapidity. Every improvement in military technique entails a reorganisation and reconstruction of the military mechanism; every innovation, every expansion of the military power of one state stimulates all the others. What we observe here is like the phenomenon we come across in the sphere of tariff policies where a raise of rates in one state is immediately

[1] O. Schwarz: "Finanzen der Gegenwart," in *Handwörterbuch der Staatswissenschaften*. It must be noted that the author's figures of German and Austrian expenditures are incorrect, for they do not include the extraordinary budgets and the appropriations made only once; the figures for the U.S.A. do not include the "civil expenditure" of the individual states, so that the increase (33.5–56.9) is in reality much larger.

[2] We quote from *The Statesman's Yearbook* for 1915.

reflected in all others, causing a general raise. Of course, here, too, we have before us only a case of a general principle of competition, for the military power of the state capitalist trust is the weapon to be used in its economic struggle. The growth of armaments, creating as it does a demand for the products of the metallurgic industry, raises substantially the importance of heavy industry, particularly the importance of "cannon kings" à la Krupp. To say, however, that wars are *caused* by the ammunition industry,[1] would be a cheap assertion. The ammunition industry is by no means a branch of production existing for itself, it is not an artificially created evil which in turn calls forth the "battle of nations." It ought to be obvious from the foregoing considerations that armaments are an indispensable attribute of state power, an attribute that has a very definite function in the struggle among state capitalist trusts. Capitalist society is unthinkable without armaments, as it is unthinkable without wars. And just as it is true that not low prices cause competition but, on the contrary, competition causes low prices, it is equally true that not the existence of arms is the prime cause and the moving force in wars (although wars are obviously impossible without arms) but, on the contrary, the inevitableness of economic conflicts conditions the existence of arms. This is why in our times, when economic conflicts have reached an unusual degree of intensity, we are witnessing a mad orgy of armaments. Thus the rule of finance capital implies both imperialism and militarism. In this sense militarism is no less a typical historic phenomenon than finance capital itself.

With the growth of the importance of state power, its inner structure also changes. The state becomes more than ever before an "executive committee of the ruling classes." It is true that state power always reflected the interests of the "upper strata,"[2] but inasmuch as the top layer itself was a

---

[1] *Cf.* the above mentioned book by Pavlovich. A more shallow variety of this theory is advanced by Kautsky when he asserts (in his *Nationalstaat, imperialistischer Staat und Staatenbund*, also in numerous articles in the *Neue Zeit* during the war) that the war was caused—by mobilisation. This is, indeed, putting things on their heads.

[2] This is recognised also by a few burgeois sociologists and economists. *Franz Oppenheimer*, for instance, views the state as the organisation of the classes that own the means of production (in the first place the land) utilised

more or less amorphous mass, the organised state apparatus faced an unorganised class (or classes) whose interests it embodied. Matters are totally different now. The state apparatus not only embodies the interests of the ruling classes in general, but also their collectively expressed will. It faces no more atomised members of the ruling classes, but their organisations. Thus the government is *de facto* transformed into a "committee" elected by the representatives of entrepreneurs' organisations, and it becomes the highest guiding force of the state capitalist trust. This is one of the main causes of the so-called crises of parliamentarism. In former times parliament served as an arena for the struggle among various factions of the ruling groups (bourgeoisie and landowners, various strata of the bourgeoisie among themselves, etc.). Finance capital has consolidated almost all of their varieties into one "solid reactionary mass" united in many centralised organisations. "Democratic" and "liberal" sentiments are replaced by open monarchist tendencies in modern imperialism, which is always in need of a state dictatorship. Parliament at present serves more as a decorative institution; it passes upon decisions prepared beforehand in the businessmen's organisations and gives only formal sanction to the collective will of the consolidated bourgeoisie as a whole. A "strong power" has become the ideal of the modern bourgeois. These sentiments are not "remnants of feudalism," as some observers suppose, these are not débris of the old that have survived in our times. This is an entirely new socio-political formation caused by the growth of finance capital. If the old feudal "policy of blood and iron" was able to serve here, externally, as a model, this was possible only because the moving springs of modern economic life drive capital along the road of aggressive politics and the militarisation of all social life. The best proof may be found not only in the foreign policies of such "democratic" countries as Eng-

to exploit the masses of the people. His formula to a certain degree approaches the Marxian theory—with modifications that impair its value (placing the emphasis on the "land," etc.). It is a curious incident that in polemic notes against Oppenheimer such an authority of German sociology and economics as Adolf Wagner admits to a large extent the correctness of Oppenheimer's formula, referring it, however, to the "historic" (!) state. See his article, "Staat in nationalökonomischer Hinsicht," in *Handwörterbuch der Staatswissenschaften*, 3rd edition, Vol. 7, p. 731.

land, France, Belgium (note the colonial policy of Belgium), and the United States, but also in the changes that take place in their internal policies (militarisation and the growth of monarchism in France, the increasing attempts at attacking the freedom of labour organisations in all countries, etc., etc.).

Being a very large shareholder in the state capitalist trust, the modern state is the highest and all-embracing organisational culmination of the latter. Hence its colossal, almost monstrous, power.

PART IV

THE FUTURE OF IMPERIALISM AND WORLD ECONOMY

CHAPTER XII

"Necessity" of Imperialism, and "Ultra-imperialism"

1. CONCEPTION OF HISTORIC NECESSITY. HISTORIC NECESSITY AND PRACTICAL MARXISM. HISTORIC "NECESSITY" OF IMPERIALISM. 2. THE ECONOMIC APPROACH TO THE PROBLEM OF ULTRA-IMPERIALISM (AGREEMENT BETWEEN THE STATE CAPITALIST TRUSTS). ABSTRACT ECONOMIC POSSIBILITY OF A WORLD TRUST. 3. CONCRETE PROGNOSIS. ECONOMIC CONDITIONS UNDER WHICH TRUSTS ARE FORMED, AND THEIR STABILITY. INTERNATIONALISATION AND NATIONALISATION OF CAPITALIST INTERESTS. WHAT IMPERIALIST POLICIES MEAN TO THE BOURGEOISIE. 4. OVERCOMING OF IMPERIALISM AND CONDITION UNDER WHICH THIS OVERCOMING IS POSSIBLE.

Tout comprendre—c'est tout pardonner [1] says a French adage. Not every adage, however, expresses a correct thought. In this instance we deal with an obviously incorrect idea. To understand a phenomenon means to establish a causal relation between it and another phenomenon or series of phenomena. From this it does not at all follow that a phenomenon correctly understood must be forgiven under all circumstances. If this were so, then all phenomena labelled as "evil" in the language of "ethical personalities" are forever closed to human reason: since evil cannot be forgiven, obviously it cannot be understood. In reality matters are not as bad as that. On the contrary, only then can we appraise a phenomenon, *i.e.*, characterise it as positive or negative, when we understand it. Consequently, even when we are by no means inclined to "forgive," we must first of all "understand." This elementary truth is applicable also to historic events. To understand an historic event means to represent it as the consequence of a definite historic cause or historic causes; in other words, to represent it not as an "accidental" entity caused by nothing,

[1] To understand everything, is to forgive everything.—*Ed.*

130

but as an entity inevitably flowing from the total of given conditions. The element of causality is the element of necessity ("causal necessity"). Marxism teaches us that the historic process, and consequently every link in the chain of historic events, is a "necessary" entity. To deduce political fatalism from this doctrine is absurd, for the simple reason that historic events are taking place not outside of but through the will of people, through the class struggle if we deal with a class society. The will of the classes is in every instance determined by given circumstances; in this respect it is not at all "free." However, that will becomes in turn a conditioning factor of the historic process. If we eliminate the actions of people, the struggle of classes, etc., we eliminate the entire historic process. *Fatalist* "Marxism" has always been a bourgeois-made caricature of the Marxist doctrine, contrived by the theoreticians of the ruling class in order more easily to overcome Marxism. We have all heard the widely circulated sophism that Marxists predicting the inevitable coming of the post-capitalist order are like a party struggling for the coming of a lunar eclipse. On the other hand there has been a strong tendency among bourgeois opportunists, when they sought for a "strictly scientific" formulation of their desires, to wrap themselves in the cloak of that "Marxism," which, to them, elevates everything existing at a given moment to the rank of the absolute, and sees in the existing a limit that cannot be overstepped. Hegel's formula, "Everything that is is reasonable," was more than once utilised by such opportunists for their own purpose. Whereas for Marx the "reasonableness of everything existing" was only the expression of a causal relation between the present and the past, a relation the understanding of which is the starting point for the *overcoming* of the "existing," this "reasonableness" served for the opportunists to justify and perpetuate it.[1] *Die Geschichte hat immer Recht*, (history is always right), this is how a "Marxist," Heinrich Cunow, justifies his "acceptance" of imperialism.[2]

[1] Marx once made a caustic remark about the "historic school" saying that "history reveals itself to them, as Jehovah, the God of Israel, to Moses, only *a posteriori*." This hits directly at the present-day renegades of Marxism.
[2] *Cf.* Heinrich Cunow: *Parteizusammenbruch? Ein offenes Wort zum inneren Parteistreit*, Berlin, 1915.

Every idea of overcoming it, he says, is only an "illusion"; the desire to systematise such ideas is a "worship of illusions" (*Illusionenkultus*). Of course, nothing is more shallow than such an interpretation of Marxism. An excellent reply to Cunow is contained in Marx's answer to the bourgeois economist, Burke.

"The laws of commerce" (the latter said) "are the laws of nature and therefore the laws of God," to which Marx replied: "In view of the abominable lack of principle that we see on all hands to-day, and in view of the devout faith in 'the laws of commerce,' it is our boundless duty again and again to stigmatise the Burkes whose only difference from their successors was that they had talent!" [1]

But if things existing historically are subject to various estimations, what is it then that determines "practice"? Where are the limits of the achievable?   To answer these questions more fully let us suppose two extreme cases.   Let us first assume that we are dealing with a feebly developed proletariat in a country that has only just started on the road of capitalist development.   The social classes in such a country still represent an unorganised mass.   The proletariat itself has not yet become what Marx terms a "class for itself." The economic development is so weak that there are no objective conditions for the organisation of the economic life on a social scale.   In such a case, we can say outright that there is an absence of prerequisites necessary for the overcoming of capitalist contradictions.   While recognising in principle the conditional existence of capitalism, the Marxists at the same time point out that once it is impossible to divert social development from the capitalist tracks, what remains to be done is to reckon with the future of capitalist development and to organise the forces for the active overcoming of capitalism in the future, utilising at present the comparative progressiveness of the latter, fighting against the remnants of feudalism that hamper social progress, etc.   There are, consequently, two decisive moments determining the foundations of "practical activity": First an "analysis of objective conditions," *i.e.*, of a given state of economic development; second, an analysis of

[1] *Capital*, Vol. I, p. 843.

the specific social weight of the progressive social force itself, which of course is connected with the first moment. It is under conditions just pictured that Marxists speak of the necessity of capitalism, meaning the relative impossibility of overcoming it.

Let us now assume, secondly, that we deal with a highly developed capitalist organism, which makes the introduction of a planned course of social production possible; let us also assume the interrelation of social forces to be such that a considerable portion of the population belongs to the most progressive class. Under such conditions it is perfectly absurd to place the emphasis on capitalism as the "necessary" stage of development. (The latter to be understood not in the sense that capitalism as well as its present stage are products of historic development, but in the sense that it cannot be overcome.)[1]

If we now approach the question of the necessity of imperialism (the impossibility of overcoming it), we realise at once that there is no ground whatever to treat its necessity in this sense. On the contrary, imperialism is the policy of finance capitalism, i.e., a highly developed capitalism implying a considerable ripeness of the organisation of production; in other words, imperialist policies by their very existence bespeak the ripeness of the objective conditions for a new socioeconomic form; consequently, all talk about the "necessity" of imperialism as a limit to action is liberalism, is in itself semi-imperialism. The further existence of capitalism and imperialism becomes nothing more nor less than a question of the interrelation between mutually struggling class forces.

There exists, however, the danger of another opportunist deviation, which is outwardly opposed to fatalism—a theory now being most assiduously developed in literature by Karl Kautsky.[2] Starting from the correct notion that the further

[1] We have seen that the *absolute* impossibility of overcoming capitalism does not exist for Marxists. When, however, there is a *relative* impossibility (e.g., capitalism in its initial stages), Marxists by no means undertake to "cultivate" capitalism, "to serve as apprentices in the capitalist system." This they leave to the Struves *et tutti quanti*. The Marxists will find other tasks.

[2] Karl Kautsky: *Nationalstaat, imperialistischer Staat und Staatenbund,* also articles in the *Neue Zeit* for 1914-15. It must be noted that even earlier Kautsky took the point of view discussed in the text below. Such, for instance, was his stand on "disarmament."

existence of imperialism depends upon the interrelation of social forces, Kautsky proceeds along the following line.

Imperialism, he says, is a definite method of capitalist politics; the latter can exist even without forcible methods, in the same way as capitalism can exist with an eight-hour work day instead of a ten- or twelve-hour day. As far as the work day is concerned, the proletariat meets the bourgeois tendency towards increasing the labour day with its proletarian tendency to shorten the number of labour hours, doing so within the framework of capitalism. In the very same manner, says Kautsky, it is necessary to meet the bourgeois violent tendencies of imperialism with the peaceful tendencies of the proletariat. Thus, Kautsky asserts, the question can be solved within the framework of capitalism. Radical as this theory may seem at the first glance, it is in fact a thoroughly reformist one. Later we shall deal at length with the analysis of the possibility of "peaceful capitalism" $à$ la Kautsky ("ultra-imperialism"). At present we wish to advance only a formal argument. We assert, namely, that from the fact that imperialism is a problem of the interrelation of forces, it does not at all follow that it can disappear within the framework of capitalism, just as the fifteen-hour work day or unregulated wages, etc., disappeared. If the problem were to be solved so simply, it would be possible to "map out" also the following perspective: it is known that capitalism implies the acquisition of surplus value by the capitalists; all the new value n is divided into two parts, $n = v + s$; this distribution, looked upon from its quantitative side, depends upon the interrelation of social forces (the antagonism of interests was early formulated by Ricardo). With the growth of resistance on the part of the working class it is perfectly thinkable that v will increase at the expense of s, and that n will be distributed in a proportion more favourable for the workers. Since, however, the gradual increase of the proletariat's share is determined by the interrelation of forces, and since there is no limit set for this increase, the working class, having reduced the share of the capitalist to the size of mere salaries, peacefully "drains" capitalism in turning the capitalists into mere employees or— at worst—into pensioners of the collective social body. This idyllic picture is obviously a reformist Utopia. No less of a Utopia is Kautsky's "ultra-imperialism."

Kautsky and his followers assert that the very process of capitalist development is favourable to the growth of elements that can serve as a support for ultra-imperialism. The growth of international interdependence of capital, they say, creates a tendency towards eliminating competition among the various "national" capitalist groups. This "peaceful" tendency, they say, is strengthened by pressure from below, and in this way rapacious imperialism is replaced by gentle ultra-imperialism.

Let us analyse the question on its merits. Speaking economically, the question must be formulated as follows: how is an agreement (or a merger) of the state capitalist trusts possible? For imperialism, as we all know, is nothing but the expression of competition between state capitalist trusts. Once this competition disappears, the ground for the policy of imperialism disappears also, and capital divided into many "national" groups is transformed into a single world organisation, a universal world trust opposed by the world proletariat.

Speaking in an abstract, theoretical way, such a trust is perfectly thinkable, for, generally speaking, there is no economic limit to the process of cartelisation. In our opinion, Hilferding is perfectly right when, in his *Finanzkapital*, he says:

The question arises as to where the limits of cartelisation can actually be drawn. The question must be answered in the sense that there is no absolute limit to cartelisation. On the contrary, the tendency towards a continuous widening of the scope of cartelisation may be observed. Independent industries are becoming more and more dependent upon the cartelised ones, and finally join them. As a result of this process, a universal cartel ought to emerge. Here all capital production would be consciously regulated from one centre, which determines the size of production in all its spheres. . . . This would be a consciously regulated society in an antagonistic form. This antagonism, however, is the antagonism of distribution. . . . The tendency towards creating such a universal cartel, and the tendency towards establishing a central bank coincide, and out of their unification grows the great concentrating power of finance capital.[1]

[1] Rudolf Hilferding, *l.c.*, p. 295.

This abstract economic possibility, however, by no means signifies its actual probability. The same Hilferding is perfectly right when he says in another place:

> Economically, a universal cartel to guide all production and thus to eliminate crises, would be possible; such a cartel would be thinkable economically, although socially and politically such a state appears unrealisable, for the antagonism of interests, strained to the last possible limits, would necessarily bring about its collapse.[1]

In reality, however, the socio-political causes would not even admit the formation of such an all-embracing trust. In the following we shall attempt to prove this thesis.

Comparative equality of positions in the world market is the first condition for the formation of a more or less stable compact. Where there is no such equality, the group occupying a more favourable position in the world market has no reason for joining a compact: on the contrary, it sees an advantage in continuing the struggle, for it has grown to hope that the competitor will be defeated. This is a general rule for the formation of compacts. It is just as applicable to the state capitalist trusts, with which we are dealing here, as it is in other cases. Two series of conditions, however, have to be taken into consideration here.

First of all, purely economic equality. This includes equality in the cost of production. Equality in the cost of production, however, reduces itself in the final analysis to equality in labour values and therefore to a relatively equal level of development of productive forces. Thus equality of economic structure is a condition for the formation of agreements. Where the difference in economic structure is considerable, where there is, as a consequence, inequality in the cost of production, there the state capitalist trust that possesses a higher technique finds it unprofitable to enter into an agreement. This is why the highly developed industry of Germany —to take as an example the practice of agreements as we find it in the various production branches—prefers to appear isolated in the world market as far as its main lines are concerned. Of course, when we deal with a state capitalist trust, we take

[1] *Ibid.*

into account a certain mean figure relative to all the production branches; we then proceed, not from the interests of the capitalist groups owning one or the other production branch, but from the interests of "organised industry," where after all the dominant note is being struck by the large-scale capitalists of the heavy industry, whose relative economic importance keeps on growing. Transportation cost is added to production cost proper.

Aside from this "purely economic" equality, a necessary condition for the formation of stable agreements is equality of economic policies. We have seen above that capital's connection with the state is transformed into an additional economic force. The stronger state secures for its industries the most advantageous trade treaties, and establishes high tariffs that are disadvantageous for the competitors. It helps its finance capital to monopolise the sales markets, the markets for raw materials, and particularly the spheres of capital investment. It is therefore easily understood why, when conditions of the struggle are being taken stock of in the world market, the state capitalist trusts reckon not only with the purely economic conditions of the struggle but also with the economic policies of the respective states. This is why even where there are relatively equal economic structures, but the military powers of the state capitalist trusts differ considerably, it is better for the stronger to continue the struggle rather than to enter into a compact or to merge with the others. If we view the situation of the struggling "nations" from this point of vantage, we realise that there is no reason to expect, at least in the more or less near future, an agreement or a merging of the state capitalist trusts and their transformation into a single world trust. It is sufficient to compare the economic structure of France and Germany, of England and America, of the developed countries in general, with such countries as Russia (the latter, though not belonging to the category of state capitalist trusts, nevertheless add to the establishment of certain relations in the world market) to realise how far we are from a world capitalist organisation.[1] The same may

---

[1] To avoid misunderstandings, we must emphasise that this assertion of ours by no means contradicts another one which says that the economic development of the foremost countries has created "objective prerequisites" for

be said also as regards military power. If the present war has shown (at least so far) a comparative equality of the opposing groups, one must not forget that we deal here with combinations of forces, each of which is by no means a stable entity.

The question of equality must be considered not only statically, but mainly dynamically. The "national" groups of the bourgeoisie build their plans not only on what "is" but also on what "will probably be." They take into strict account every possibility of development which may allow a certain group to become superior to all the others in due time, although at the present moment it may be economically and politically equal to its competitor. This circumstance makes the lack of equilibrium still more actue.[1] The great stimulus to the formation of an international state capitalist trust is given by the internationalisation of capitalist interests as described in the first section of our work (participation in and financing of international enterprises, international cartels, trusts, etc.). Significant as this process may be in itself, it is, however, counteracted by a still stronger tendency of capital towards nationalisation, and towards remaining secluded within state boundaries. The benefits accruing to a "national" group of the bourgeoisie from a continuation of the struggle are much greater than the losses sustained in consequence of that struggle. By no means must we overestimate the significance of the already existing international industrial agreements. As we have noted above, many of them are very unstable, representing as they do businessmen's organisations of a relatively low type with a comparatively small centralisation, and often embracing highly specialised production branches (the bottle syndicate). Only companies formed in such spheres of

the social organisation of production. As far as the possibility of social production is concerned, the foremost countries are all on a comparatively equal level. There is no contradiction between those assertions, because the basis of differentiation is not the same.

[1] The bourgeoisie understands this perfectly well. Thus, a German professor, Max Krahmann (in his book, *Krieg und Montanindustrie*, Berlin, 1915, first volume of the series, *Krieg und Volkswirtschaft*) says: "As in the present small [!] World War, so in the future great war, where North America and Eastern Asia will also have their word to say, it is entirely impossible for the group of agricultural states to fight the union of industrial states. . . . Thus, universal peace [*der Weltfrieden*] could be secured, were the industrial states able to come to terms [*sich vertragen könnten*]. Since this is excluded for the time being, then . ." etc. (p. 15).

production as are based on a natural monopoly (oil) possess comparative stability. Of course, the tendency towards internationalisation would none the less triumph "in the last analysis," but it would do so after a considerable period of very stubborn struggles between the state capitalist trusts.

But are not the costs of the struggle, *i.e.*, military expenditures, perchance so large that it does not pay for the bourgeoisie to continue in this way? Is not such a plan as the proposed militarisation of England an expression of bourgeois "stupidity" which is blind to its own interests? Alas, it is not so. We must attribute this quality rather to the naïve pacifists than to the bourgeoisie. The latter keeps its balance sheet in perfect shape. The truth of the matter is that those who make such arguments ordinarily lose sight of all the complex functions of military power. Such power, as we have seen above, functions not only in times of war but also in times of peace, to back up its finance capital in "peaceful competition." The pacifists forget that the war burdens, due to the incidence of taxation, etc., are borne mainly by the working class, partly by the intermediary economic groupings which are being expropriated during the war (which means in the process of the greatest centralisation of production).

It follows from the above that the actual process of economic development will proceed in the midst of a sharpened struggle between the state capitalist trusts and the backward economic formations. A series of wars is unavoidable. In the historic process which we are to witness in the near future, world capitalism will move in the direction of a universal state capitalist trust by absorbing the weaker formations. Once the present war is over, new problems will have to be "solved" by the sword. Partial agreements are, of course, possible here and there (*e.g.*, the fusion of Germany and Austria is quite probable). Every agreement or fusion, however, will only reproduce the bloody struggle on a new scale. Were "Central Europe" to unite according to the plans of the German imperialists, the situation would remain comparatively the same; but even were *all* of Europe to unite, it would not yet signify "disarmament." It would signify an unheard of rise of militarism because the problem to be solved would be a colossal struggle between Europe on the one hand, America and Asia on the other. The struggle among small (small!) state capitalist trusts would be replaced by a struggle between still more colossal trusts. To attempt to eliminate this struggle by "home remedies" and rose water is tantamount to bombarding an elephant with peas, for imperialism is not only a system most intimately connected with modern capitalism, it is also the most essential element of the latter.

We have seen in the second section the peculiarities in the structure of modern capitalism and the formation of state capitalist trusts. This economic structure, however, is connected with a certain policy, namely, the imperialist policy. This not only in the sense that imperialism is a product of finance capitalism, but also in the sense that finance capital cannot pursue any other policy than an imperialist one, as we characterised it above. The state capitalist trust cannot become an adherent of free trade for thereby it would lose a considerable part of its capitalist *raison d'être*. We have already pointed out that protectionism allows the acquisition of additional profits on the one hand, facilitates competition in the world market on the other. In the same way finance capital, expressing as it does capitalist monopoly organisations, cannot relinquish the policy of monopolising "spheres of influence," of seizing sales markets and markets for raw materials, or spheres of capital investment. If one state capitalist trust fails to get hold of an unoccupied territory, it will be occupied by another. Peaceful rivalry, which corresponded to the epoch of free competition and of the absence of any organisation of production at home, is absolutely inconceivable in the epoch of an entirely different production structure and of the struggle among state capitalist trusts. Those imperialist interests are of such magnitude for the finance capitalist groups, and they are so connected with the very foundations of their existence, that the governments do not shrink before the most colossal military expenditures only to secure for themselves a stable position in the world market. The idea of "disarmament" within the framework of capitalism is particularly absurd as far as the state capitalist trusts that occupy the foremost positions in the world market are concerned. Before their eyes there always shines the picture of subjugating the whole world, of acquiring an unheard of field for exploitation—a thing termed by the French imperialists *l'organisation d'économie mondiale* and by the German imperialists, *Organisierung der Weltwirtschaft*. Would the bourgeoisie exchange this "high" ideal for the pot of porridge of disarmament? Where is the guarantee for a given state capitalist trust that a pernicious rival will not continue the "abandoned" policy in spite of all formal agreements and guarantees? Everyone acquainted with the history of the struggle among cartels even within the boundaries of one country knows how often, when the situation changed, when the market conditions changed, agreements dissolved like soap bubbles. Imagine a strong state capitalist trust like the U. S. waging war against a union of all other trusts—the "agreement" will then be shattered to pieces in no time. (In the latter case we would have a tremendous formation constructed after the type of an ordinary syndicate, and having the state capitalist trusts as its component parts. Such an agreement between the state capitalist trusts would not be able at once to skip all intermediary stages, to become a real centralised trust. A type of agreement, however, that implies intense internal struggle is easily amenable to the influence of changing conditions.) We have taken a hypothetical case where formal unification is a fact. However, this unification cannot take place because the bourgeoisie of every country is by no means as naïve as many of its *bona fide* pacifists who wish nothing more than to persuade the bourgeoisie and to "prove" to it that it does not understand its own advantages. . . .

But, one may argue, this is exactly what Kautsky and his friends assume, namely, that the bourgeoisie will relinquish its imperialistic methods when it is compelled to do so by pressure from below. Our reply is that two possibilities are open in this case: either the pressure is weak, then everything remains as before; or the pressure is stronger than the "resistance," then we have before us not a new era of ultra-imperialism but a new era of non-antagonistic social development.

The entire structure of world economy in our times forces

the bourgeoisie to pursue an imperialist policy. As the colonial policy is inevitably connected with violent methods, so every capitalist expansion leads sooner or later to a bloody climax. "Violent methods," says Hilferding, "are inseparably bound up with the very essence of colonial policy, which without them would lose its capitalist meaning; they are so much an integral element of the colonial policy as the existence of a proletariat divorced from all ownership is generally a *conditio sine qua non* of capitalism. To be in favour of a colonial policy and at the same time to talk about eliminating its violent methods, is a dream which cannot be treated with more ear-nestness than the illusion that one can eliminate the proletariat while retaining capitalism." [1]

The same thing may be said about imperialism. It is an integral element of finance capitalism without which the latter would lose its capitalist meaning. To imagine that the trusts, this embodiment of monopoly, have become the bearers of the free trade policy, of peaceful expansion, is a deeply harmful Utopian fantasy.

But is not the epoch of "ultra-imperialism" a real possibility after all, can it not be affected by the centralisation process? Will not the state capitalist trusts devour one another gradually until there comes into existence an all-embracing power which has conquered all the others? This possibility would be thinkable if we were to look at the social process as a purely mechanical one, without counting the forces that are hostile to the policy of imperialism. In reality, however, the wars that will follow each other on an ever larger scale must inevitably result in a shifting of the social forces. The centralisation process, looked at from the capitalist angle, will inevitably clash with a socio-political tendency that is antagonistic to the former. Therefore it can by no means reach its logical end; it suffers collapse and achieves completion only in a new, purified, non-capitalist form. It is for this reason that Kautsky's theory is by no means realisable. It looks upon imperialism not as an inevitable accompaniment of capi-list development, but as upon one of the "dark sides" of capitalist development. Like Proudhon, whose philistine

[1] Hilferding, *l.c.*, p. 401.

Utopia Marx fought so bitterly, Kautsky wishes to eliminate "dark" imperialism leaving intact the "sunny" sides of the capitalist order. His concept implies a slurring over of the gigantic contradictions which rend asunder modern society, and in this respect it is a reformist concept. It is a characteristic feature of theorising reformism that it takes pains to point out all the elements of capitalism's adaptation to conditions without seeing its contradictions. For a consistent Marxist, the entire development of capitalism is nothing but a process of a continuous reproduction of the contradictions of capitalism on an ever wider scale. The future of world economy, as far as it is a capitalist economy, will not overcome its inherent lack of adaptation; on the contrary, it will keep on reproducing this lack of adaptation on an ever wider scale. These contradictions are actually harmonised in another production structure of the social organism—through a well-planned Socialist organisation of economic activities.

CHAPTER XIII

War and Economic Evolution

1. CHANGE IN THE ECONOMIC RELATIONS AMONG STATE CAPITALIST TRUSTS (INCREASED IMPORTANCE OF AMERICA; ELIMINATION OF SMALL STATES). 2. WORLD ECONOMY AND ECONOMIC AUTARCHY. 3. CHANGE IN THE INNER STRUCTURE OF STATE CAPITALIST TRUSTS (DISAPPEARANCE OF INTERMEDIARY GROUPS, GROWTH OF POWER OF FINANCE CAPITAL, GROWTH OF STATE INTERFERENCE, STATE MONOPOLIES, ETC.). 4. STATE CAPITALISM AND SHARPENING OF STRUGGLE BETWEEN STATE CAPITALIST TRUSTS. 5. STATE CAPITALISM AND THE CLASSES.

THE war, which was bound to break out because it had been prepared by the entire course of events, could not fail to exercise a colossal influence on world economic life. It has caused a complete change in every country and in the relations between countries, in the "national economies" and in world economy. Together with a truly barbarous squandering of production forces, with the destruction of the material means of production and of the living labour power, together with the devitalisation of economy through monstrous socially harmful expenditures, the war, like a gigantic crisis, has intensified the fundamental tendencies of capitalist development; it has hastened to an extraordinary degree the growth of finance capitalist relations and the centralisation of capital on a world scale. The centralising character of the present war (imperialist centralisation) is beyond doubt. First of all, there is a collapse of independent small states whether of high industrial development (horizontal concentration and centralisation) or of an agrarian type (vertical centralisation); the latter have also absorbed some of the weaker (and similarly backward) formations—which, however, is comparatively unimportant. The independent existence of Belgium, a highly developed country with a colonial policy of its own, is becoming doubtful; the process of a centralising redivision of territory in the Balkans is perfectly obvious; it is to be expected that the

tangle of colonial possessions in Africa will be straightened
out. On the other hand, we witness a very strong rapproche-
ment (in the form of a lasting agreement between syndicates)
of Germany and Austria-Hungary. Whatever the actual outcome of the war, it is already clear (and could have been assumed *a priori*) that the political map will be changed in the
direction of greater state homogeneity—this being exactly the
way in which the imperialistic "nationality states" (*Nationali-
tätenstaaten*) grow.

If the general tendency of development, only intensified by
the war, consists in a further process of centralisation, the war
has also considerably accelerated the appearance on the world
arena of one of the largest state capitalist trusts, possessed of
an unusually strong internal organisation. We mean the
United States of America.

The war has placed the United States in an unprecedented,
exclusive position. With the cessation of the Russian grain
export, etc., to Europe, the demand for American agrarian
products has increased; on the other hand, there is a stupendous demand for the products of the war industry of the
United States on the part of the belligerent countries.[1] To the
United States is also directed the quest for credit capital
(foreign loans, etc.). Only recently America was a debtor to
Europe; in consequence of the war the situation changes
rapidly: America's debts are being repaid, and in the field of
current accounts and short term credits America is becoming
the creditor of Europe. This growing financial importance of
the United States has another no less significant side to it.
The secondary American states used to import capital from
Europe, mainly from England and France, while the import
of capital from the United States, itself an importer of European capital, was of little importance. During the war,
however, Canada, Argentina, Panama, Bolivia, and Costa Rica

[1] The growth of American export for the first four months of 1915 compared with the first four months of 1914, may be seen from the following
figures (in millions of dollars): January, 1914, 204.2; January, 1915, 267.9;
February, 173.9 and 299.8 respectively; March, 187.5 and 296.5 respectively;
April, 162.5 and 294.5 (*Vestnik Finansov*, No. 16). Mr. Pratt, the head of
the Bureau of Foreign and Domestic Commerce, characteristically remarked that
the country faced a new period wherein the expression "domestic market"
would seem archaic compared with the slogan of a world market (*Vestnik
Finansov*, No. 16).

have placed their loans not in Europe but in the United States. "The American countries have received small sums, but what is characteristic in this transaction is the fact that the enumerated countries had usually been clients of the London market. Thus New York has replaced London for the time of the war and has, as it were, given impetus to the realisation of the financial section of a Pan-American programme.[1] The continuation of the war, the payments for war orders and loans, later the immense demand for capital in the post-war period (when the reconstruction of fixed capital will have to be undertaken, etc.) will increase the financial importance of the United States still more. It will hasten the accumulation of American capital; it will widen its sphere of influence in the rest of America, and will rapidly make the United States a prime factor in the world struggle for markets.[2]

The example of the United States of America shows how a large state capitalist trust grows and becomes consolidated, how it absorbs countries and territories formerly dependent upon Europe. Simultaneously with the extension of America's world connections, we witness a highly intensive progress of "national consolidation." Stronger still are the "nationalising" tendencies inside of the belligerent groups: international commodity exchange has been disrupted, the movement of capital and labour power from one belligerent country to the other has ceased, nearly all relations have been severed. Within the boundaries of "national" economy (of which the best example is Germany, for Germany is cut off from the rest of the world most completely) there goes on a hasty redistribution of productive forces. This relates not only to the war industry (it is a well known fact that even piano factories in Germany have been adapted to new tasks, namely, they manufacture shells), but also to foodstuffs and agriculture in general. Thus the war has unusually intensified the tendency towards economic autarchy, towards transforming the "national" economy into a self-sufficient whole, more or less isolated from world

[1] M. Bogolepov: "American Capital Market," in *Vestnik Finansov*, 1915, No. 39, p. 501. *Cf.* his articles on the same subject in *Vestnik Finansov*, Nos. 37 and 38.
[2] At the very beginning of the war, Kautsky, in the *Neue Zeit*, called attention to the growing importance of America.

connections.   Does it follow, however, that this tendency will continually prevail, that world economy will be split up into a number of independent parts entirely isolated from each other? So, or almost so, does Utopian imperialism think.   The ideologists of imperialism strive towards a state of affairs where a country produces everything "by itself," where it "does not depend upon foreigners," etc.   Let the country acquire the necessary "economic supplements," let it secure for itself the sources of raw material, and the task, they say, is achieved. Such arguments, however, will not stand the light of criticism. The imperialist gentlemen completely forget that the annexationist activities they pursue imply the growth of economic world connections, the expansion of capital and commodity export, the increase of raw materials' import, and so forth. Thus, from a certain point of view, the policy of imperialism contains a contradiction: the imperialist bourgeoisie must, on the one hand, develop world relations to a maximum (remember the dumping policy of the cartels), on the other hand, it erects a tariff wall between itself and the world; on the one hand it exports capital, on the other it cries over foreign supremacy; in a word, on the one hand it internationalises economic life, on the other hand it strives with all its might to bottle it up within "national boundaries."   Still, notwithstanding all obstacles, the basis of international connections keeps on growing, hence Felix Pinner is perfectly right when he says:

Remembering that the unusual expansion of foreign trade took place in the period of the most decisive nationalist economic policy, we must assume that the war, and the political sentiments of the great powers called forth by the war, will destroy international relations as little as this was hitherto done by the seclusion tendency [Absperrungstendenzen].[1]

While the war is going on, the disappearance or the weakening of economic connections in one place is accompanied by their growth in another.   The dominant rôle played by the Germans in Russia has been discontinued, only to give place to the dominant rôle of the Entente powers.   Nor is this all.

[1] Felix Pinner: "Die Konjunktur des wirtschaftlichen Sozialismus," in Die Bank, April, 1915.

We must remember that the regulative principle of capitalist activity is the accumulation of profits. War is one of the "business operations" of the modern bourgeois; once it is over, he is as eager as of yore to establish old connections (not to speak of contraband operations during the war itself). Capitalist interest imperatively dictates these steps. The international division of labour, the difference in natural and social conditions, are an economic *prius* which cannot be destroyed, even by the World War. This being so, there exist definite value relations and, as their consequence, conditions for the realisation of a maximum of profit in international transactions. Not economic self-sufficiency, but an intensification of international relations, accompanied by a simultaneous "national" consolidation and ripening of new conflicts on the basis of world competition—such is the road of future evolution.

Thus if the war cannot halt the general development of world capital, if, on the contrary, it expresses the greatest expansion of the centralisation process, the war also influences the structure of individual "national" economies in such a way as to intensify centralisation within the limits of every "national" body and, while wasting productive forces on a colossal scale, it organises "national economy" in that it places it more and more under the combined rule of finance capital and the state.

In its influence on economic life, the war in many respects recalls to mind industrial crises, differing from the latter only by a greater intensity of social convulsions and devastations. Those devastations express themselves economically, first of all, in the dying out of the middle strata of the bourgeoisie—a process that goes on also during industrial crises. When markets are lost, entire branches of production perish; due to the absence of a solvent demand, connections hitherto firmly rooted are disrupted, the entire credit system is shaken, etc. Outside of the workers, however, the most afflicted elements are the middle strata of the bourgeoisie: they go bankrupt first of all. Large-scale cartel industry, on the contrary, does not feel unhappy at all. It is easy to gather abundant statistical material to illustrate the rise in the profits of a whole series of the largest enterprises, particularly such enterprises as are close to army deliveries, *i.e.*, in the first place enterprises in the sphere of heavy industries (so-called "military profits").   In spite of the fact that the sum total of surplus value produced does not grow (on the contrary, it is diminishing, due to the fact that a vast number of hands are diverted to the army), the profits of the large-scale bourgeois groups keep on growing. This goes on to a large extent at the expense of the profits of other, small and uncartelised, groups of the bourgeoisie.   (This increase in profits is, on the other hand, explained by the rise in the value of paper securities as a draft on the future.)   Where there is a colossal expenditure of productive forces, where the fixed capital of society is being "consumed," [1] there is evident a shifting of groups and a relative growth of the large-scale bourgeois categories. This tendency will not be ended with the war. If the large-scale bourgeoisie defends and fortifies its position during the war, the post-war gigantic demands for capital will facilitate the rapid growth of large-scale banks, and consequently the rapid growth of centralisation and concentration of capital.   A feverish process of healing the wounds inflicted by the war will ensue: reconstruction of destroyed or wornout railways, shops and factory plants, machines and apparatus, rolling stock in the field of transportation, etc.; not the least among these activities will be the mending and extending of the military state apparatus.   This will increase the demand for capital to a very high degree, and will strengthen the position of banking trusts. [2]

While the finance capitalist groups are becoming stronger, there has increased tremendously the interference of the state in economic life. [3]

Under this head comes the formation of state (production and trade) monopolies; the organisation of so-called "mixed

[1] War loans signify nothing but a consuming of the parts of capital that are being worn out; those parts are replaced by paper; the real values in their material form are wasted in a non-productive way by being fired into the air.

[2] *Cf.* Cunow: "Vom Wirtschaftsleben," in *Neue Zeit*, 33,2, No. 22 ("Der Bank- und Geldmarkt im ersten Kriegsjahr"). Also Dr. Weber: "Krieg und Banken," in *Volkswirtschaftliche Zeitfragen* (*Krieg und Volkswirtschaft*), Heft 7, 1915, p. 27.

[3] In relation to Germany, see Johann Müller: "Nationalökonomische Gesetzgebung. Die durch den Krieg hervorgerufenen Gesetze, Verordnungen, Bekanntmachungen, u.s.w.," in *Jahrbücher für Nationalökonomie und Statistik* for 1915.

enterprises" (*gemischte Betriebe*) where the state or the munic-
ipalities are partners to the enterprise, hand in hand with
private syndicates and trusts; state control over the production
process of private enterprises (obligatory production, regulation of production methods, etc.): regulation of distribution
(compulsory deliveries and acceptance of goods; organisation
of state "central distribution offices;" state warehouses for
raw materials, fuel, foodstuffs; fixing of prices; bread cards,
meat cards, etc.; prohibition of import and export of goods,
etc.); organisation of state credit; lastly, state organisation of
consumption (communal kitchens).[1]

England has established, besides, state insurance of ocean
cargoes, state guarantee of merchants' promissory notes, state
payments of sums belonging to English merchants abroad, when
they cannot be obtained at the moment, etc. Similar measures
have been introduced to a greater or lesser degree by all the
belligerent states.

The "mobilisation of industry," *i.e.*, its militarisation, was
achieved with least difficulty where the entrepreneurs' organisations, cartels, syndicates, and trusts were the strongest.
Those employers' organisations, in whose interests the war is
here undertaken, have placed all their regulating apparatus at
the service of the imperialist state, to whom they are closely
related. They have thus secured the technical-economic possibility of militarising the economic life, beginning with the
direct process of production and up to the subtleties of credit
circulation. Where industry was organised into cartels, its
"mobilisation" assumed grandiose proportions.

"Large sections of economic life (*des Erwerbslebens*)," says
Mr. Pinner about Germany, "have for decades been very
closely united, the character of their activities being almost
collective; they have absorbed a large part of the national
production and have placed it under single management: these
are the cartels and trusts." [2] The aims of industrial mobilisation as well as its significance have been stressed by the English minister, Mr. Lloyd George, when he said on June 3, in

[1] Cf. Edgar Jaffé: *"Die 'Militarisierung' unseres Wirtschaftslebens,"* in *Archiv für Sozialwissenschaft und Sozialpolitik*, 1915, Bd. 40 B, Heft 3.
[2] Pinner: "Organisierte Arbeit," in *Handels-Zeitung des Berliner Tageblatts*, Aug. 23, 1915.

Manchester, that the law relative to the defence of the realm gave the government full power over all the factories; that this law made it possible for the government to give precedence to work most urgent; that it gave the government a right to dispose of every factory, every machine, and that were a difficulty to be encountered, the ministry was well supplied with arms to make its orders effective.[1] Similar measures have been adopted also in France [2] and Russia. Aside from direct control of state power over the production of private enterprises, the war has established a number of state monopolies. In England the railways have become state property; Germany has introduced bread, potato, nitrate monopolies, etc., and has a number of others in prospect (this we shall treat later); even the coal industry is turning into a "mixed cartel" where a syndicate co-operates with the government.[3] In all these cases the government directly intervenes in the sphere of production; there is, however, another and very effective governmental intervention through credit relations. Typical for the latter is the "financial mobilisation" and related operations in Germany. Even at the beginning of the war the Reichsbank operated through a series of other large banks; later its activities in this respect were greatly augmented. The so-called "loan banks" (*Darlehenskassen*), as state institutions dependent upon the Reichsbank, soon became a very important factor in the realm of credit.[4] A tremendous importance is attached to internal military loans that are being placed among the public directly by the Reichsbank. Thus the latter, an institution endowed with exceptional importance in the economic life of Germany even before the war, has grown tremendously in importance, becoming as it did a strong centre for the attraction of available portions of capital. On the other hand, it grows also as an institution that finances the ever increasing state enterprises and other state economic organisations. The central banking institute of the government

[1] We quote from the *Vestnik Finansov*, 1915, No. 24, p. 518.
[2] *Cf.* Yves Guyot: "Les Problèmes économiques après la guerre," in *Journal des économistes*, Aug. 15, 1915.
[3] *Cf.* E. Meyer: "Die Drohung mit dem Zwangssyndikat," in *Neue Zeit*, 33,2, No. 18; also "Die Bergwerksdebatte im Reichstag," in *Handels-Zeitung des Berliner Tageblatts*, No. 435, Aug. 26.
[4] Dr. Weber: *Krieg und Banken*, p. 14.

thus becomes the "golden head" of the entire state capitalist trust.

One must not think that this evolution is confined to Germany alone. *Mutatis mutandis* the same process is taking place in all the belligerent countries (also in the *non*-belligerent ones, but to a lesser degree). We must dwell here on one question that seems to us of unusual importance, namely, on the question of state monopolies and their future.

"According to calculations," said Dr. Helfferich in the Reichstag in August of this year, "the general cost of this world war for all its participants must be estimated as equal to some 300 million marks a day, *i.e.*, to something like 100 billion marks" (Hear, Hear!). "This is such a gigantic destruction and shifting of values as world history has never known." [1] It is needless to say that the figures quoted by the "Marshal of Finance," Dr. Helfferich, give no idea as to the real "general cost of the war," for they speak only of the immediate war expenditures made by the states. However, in this connection we are interested in these particular expenditures, and it will not be out of place to quote a few more detailed figures concerning military loans. The states are also spending part of their ordinary income on the war, still the following figures may give some idea as to the size of the military expenditures. [2] We use the computations quoted in No. 44, *Vestnik Finansov* for 1915. We must emphasise, however, that the figures here quoted tell us only about the war loans of the six largest states, whereas the number of states involved in the war is twelve. Where such unprecedented expenditures are made, and for no other purpose but for the further destruction of values, the state debt must grow enor-

[1] We quote from the *Vorwärts* of Aug. 21, 1915.

[2] Those figures are insufficient also in another respect: the states resort to the printing press, *i.e.*, they issue paper money in increasing quantites, which is also an internal loan, but without interest. The table indicates that up to August, 1915, Austria-Hungary obtained some 13 billion crowns (and since the figures relating to Germany are brought up to, and include, September, 1915, one may assume that the figures concerning Austria-Hungary extend up to October), whereas the military expenditures of the Austro-Hungarian government amounted up to the end of August to nearly 18 billion crowns, and up to the end of September to more than 19 billion crowns. Obviously, there must have been some sources to cover the expenses! There is no doubt, therefore, that the figures quoted in the table are considerably below the actual ones.

WAR LOANS OF SIX BELLIGERENT POWERS

GREAT BRITAIN (in thousands of pounds sterling)*		FRANCE (in thousands of francs)		RUSSIA (in thousands of rubles)		ITALY (in thousands of lira)		GERMANY (in millions of marks)		AUSTRIA-HUNGARY (in millions of crowns)	
3.5% loan, Nov., 1914..	350,000	Bank of France loans	7,000,000	5% loan, with obligatory discount at State Bank ..	2,650,000	4.5% loan, Dec., 1914 ..	1,000,000	5% loan, Sept., 1914..	3,492	5.5% loan, Nov., 1914..	2,300
3% bonds, Mar., 1915 ..	33,600	Loans by France's Allies, discounted by treasury	530,000	5% loan, Oct., 1914 ..	500,000	5% loan, July, 1915	1,000,000	5% obligation, Sept., 1914..	1,000	6% loan, Nov., 1914..	1,170
4.5% loan, July, 1915...	585,000	3.5% loan, July, 1914..	500,000	5% loan, Feb., 1915 ..	500,000	Loans from Banca d'Italia	1,216,350	5% loan, Feb., 1915	9,103	5.5% loan, May, 1915 ..	2,780
5% American loan, Oct., 1915	50,000	Bonds	7,871,000	5.5% loan May, 1915...	1,000,000			5% loan, Sept., 1915	12,101	6% loan, June, 1915 ..	1,124
Treasury Notes	214,000	Obligations	2,241,000	4% series Aug., 1914 ..	300,000			Treasury Notes	4,304	6% loan in Germany (Gross) Nov., 1914 ..	248
		English loans ..	1,250,000	4% series, Mar., 1915 ..	300,000					Same, July, 1915...	253
		U. S. A. loans..	1,250,000	Treasury notes discounted in England	1,248,324					Current Debts..	5,112
				Same in France	234,750						
				Currency loan, April, 1915 ..	200,000						
				5.5% loan, Nov., 1915 ..	*1,000,000						
Total 1,232,600		Total 20,642,000		Total 7,933,074		Total 3,216,350		Total 30,000		Total 12,987	

* The figures quoted in the table are considerably below the actual ones.

mously and the financial organisation of the state is entirely deranged. The equilibrium is so seriously impaired that additional sources to replenish the treasury must be looked for, if the colossal expenditures which will remain even after the war (payment of interest on state loans, aid for the families of invalids, etc.) are to be covered. In Germany, to take only one country, the income of the state will have to be increased more than twice.[1] It appears impossible to cover the expenses out of the usual sources of state income (state owned enterprises, direct and indirect taxation), and the states will be compelled to extend their monopolies. The leading circles of the bourgeoisie become more and more reconciled to this idea, for in the final analysis the strength of the state is their own strength. This is what the "scientific" organ of the German banks has to say through the mouth of Dr. Felix Pinner:

The basic differences of opinion which express themselves sharply as to monopolies in general, and one or the other monopoly in particular, have disappeared over night [*über Nacht verschwunden*], and almost everybody agrees that such proposed monopolies as monopolies on alcohol, kerosene, electricity [more precisely: electric current—*N.B.*], matches, perhaps even coal, salt, potassium, tobacco, and insurance, are near realisation.[2]

Under such conditions the further expansion of monopoly tendencies is very probable. Gas production, as we know, is competing with the production of electric power, consequently a gas monopoly is also probable. More probable still is the expansion of state power over enterprises contiguous upon monopolies. When the coal industry is monopolised by the state, the production of pig iron is affected. Such examples could be quoted in large numbers. The question then arises as to whether all such proposals would not remain on paper, whether they would not encounter the resistance of the bourgeoisie.

[1] *Cf.* Adolf Braun in *Neue Zeit*, 33, 1, p. 584.
[2] Felix Pinner: "Die Konjunktur des wissenschaftlichen Sozialismus," in *Die Bank*, April, pp. 326-327. On separate monopolies in Germany, see Adolf Braun: "Elektrizitätsmonopol," in *Neue Zeit*, 1915, Nos. 19 and 20; also Edmund Fischer: "Das Werden des Elektrizitätsmonopols," in *Sozialistische Monatshefte*, p. 443 *ff.*; partly Kautsky: "Zur Frage der Steuern und Monopole," *Neue Zeit*, 1914-15, I, p. 682 *ff.*

We have just indicated the change of tone in relation to state monopolies. Of course, even now there are sub-classes of the bourgeoisie, whose interests are clashing in one or the other respect. It is a fact, however, that economic evolution, fortified at this point by the war, must and does lead to a situation where the bourgeoisie as a whole is more tolerant regarding monopolistic interference of the state power. The basic reason for this change is the ever growing closeness between state power and the leading spheres of finance capital. State and private monopoly enterprises merge into one entity within the framework of the state capitalist trust. The interests of the state and the interests of finance capital coincide more and more. On the other hand, a maximum of centralisation and a maximum of state power are required by the fierce competitive struggle on the world market. The latter two causes on the one hand, and fiscal consideration on the other, form the main factors making for state organisation of production within capitalist society.

The bourgeoisie loses nothing from shifting production from one of its hands into another, since present-day state power is nothing but an entrepreneurs' company of tremendous power, headed even by the same persons that occupy the leading positions in the banking and syndicate offices. The difference is that, under such conditions, the bourgeoisie receives its income, not from the office of a syndicate, but from the office of state banks. On the other hand, the bourgeoisie is gaining from such a shift, since only when production is centralised and militarised, i.e., organised by the state, can the bourgeoisie hope to emerge victorious out of the bloody combat. Present-day war needs more than mere financial "funding." A successful war requires that factories and plants, mines and agriculture, banks and stock exchanges—everything should "work" for the war. "Everything for the war," is the slogan of the bourgeoisie. The exigencies of the war, and of imperialist preparations for war, force the bourgeoisie to adopt a new form of capitalism, to place production and distribution under state power, to destroy completely old bourgeois individualism.

Of course, not all war time measures will remain after the

war. Such measures as bread and meat rations, the ban on the production of a number of commodities, the ban on exports, etc., will disappear with the conclusion of peace. There is no doubt, however, that the tendency of the state to take hold of production will keep on increasing. Co-operation between the state and private capitalist monopolies after the type of "mixed enterprises" will probably be introduced in a number of industries; in military industries, the purely state type of production will probably remain. Cunow very correctly defines the future of the national economies as "domination of banking financiers, growth of international concentration, increase of state control and state enterprises."[1]

The processes of industrial organisation and of the increase in the economic activities of the state raises the general question as to the social meaning of this—to use Professor Jaffé's expression—change in the very principle of the economic structure. So-called State Socialists, whose adherents are recruited mainly from the councils of the German university professors, were the first to feel a rise of spirits. Karl Ballod in full earnestness speaks of the rebirth of Utopia, assuming as he does that state monopolies, etc., by themselves introduce a new structure of production.[2] Jaffé says that the militarisation of economic life differs from Socialism mainly in that the term "Socialism" is connected with the "eudemonistic trend of thought," whereas in war the individual is entirely given to the service of the "whole."[3] In the writings of Professor Krahmann we find a very curious argumentation. The future of the mining industry is thus visualised by the professor:

The present powerful effect of all the measures in support of the state and in defence of the country, introduced by the state power because of military considerations, brings us, in the sphere of mining as well as elsewhere, considerably nearer to State Socialism. The road, however, is not that which, prior to the war, was feared

[1] H. Cunow: "Die Weltwirtschaftgestaltung nach dem Kriege," in *Correspondenzblatt der Generalkommission der Gewerkschaften Deutschlands*, Sept. 11, 1915, No. 37. Cunow arrives at a wholely incorrect liberal conclusion in this article.

[2] Karl Ballod: "Einiges aus der Utopienliteratur der letzten Jahre," in *Archiv für die Geschichte des Sozialismus und der Arbeiterbewegung*, herausgegeben von Grünberg, 6. Jg. Heft I, pp. 117-118.

[3] Jaffé, *l.c.*, p. 523.

by some, expected by others. This is not internationally diluted but nationally consolidated Socialism. Such a Socialism we now approach. This is not democratic Communism, less so aristocratic class domination, but it is a nationalism that reconciles the classes. Since August 1, 1914, we have been approaching it with gigantic strides, such as would have been formerly considered entirely impossible.[1]

What is that picture of present-day "State Socialism" which appears to be a "change in principle"? From the foregoing analysis the answer seems to follow with irresistible logic: We have here the process of accelerated centralisation within the framework of a state capitalist trust, which has developed to the highest form, not of State Socialism, but of State Capitalism. By no means do we see here a new structure of production, *i.e.*, a change in the interrelation of classes; on the contrary, we have here an increase in the potency of the power of a class that owns the means of production in quantities hitherto unheard of. To apply to such a state of affairs a terminology fit for post-capitalist relations, is not only very risky, but also highly absurd. "War Socialism" and "State Socialism" are purposely being circulated with the direct intention of misleading the people and of covering up by a "good" word a very ungainly *content*. The capitalist mode of production is based on a monopoly of the means of production in the hands of the class of capitalists within the general framework of commodity exchange. There is no difference in principle whatsoever whether the state power is a direct expression of this monopoly or whether the monopoly is "privately" organised. In either case there remains commodity economy (in the first place the world market) and, what is more important, the class relations between the proletariat and the bourgeoisie.[2]

---

[1] Max Krahman: *Krieg and Montanindustrie*, pp. 22-23. The opposite view is maintained by Liefmann (see his *Stehen wir dem Sozialismus näher?*). His book is generally directed against illusions; this he does not wish to conceal.

[2] Were the commodity character of production to disappear (for instance, through the organisation of all world economy as one gigantic state trust, the impossibility of which we tried to prove in our chapter on ultra-imperialism) we would have an entirely new economic form. This would be capitalism no more, for the production of *commodities* would have disappeared; still less would it be *socialism*, for the power of one class over the other would have remained (and even grown stronger). Such an economic structure would, most of all, resemble a slaveowning economy where the slave market is absent.

It follows from the above that (as far as capitalism will retain its foothold) the future belongs to economic forms that are close to state capitalism. This further evolution of the state capitalist trusts, highly accelerated by the war, is reflected, in its turn, in the world-wide struggle among state capitalist trusts. We have seen above how the tendency to turn capitalist states into state capitalist trusts found its reflection in the mutual relations of the states. Monopoly tendencies within the "national" body have called forth tendencies to monopolise territories *outside* the home state by means of annexations; this has sharpened competition and its forms terrifically. With the further progress of internal centralisation, this acute situation will become more acute by leaps and bounds. Added to this is the rapid narrowing of the free field for capital activities. There is, therefore, not the slightest doubt that the near future will be fraught with the most cruel conflicts, and that the social atmosphere will not cease being saturated with war electricity. One of the outward expressions of this circumstance is the extraordinary growth of militarism and of imperialist sentiment. England, the land of "freedom" and "individualism," has already established a tariff and is organising a standing army; its state budget is being militarised. America is preparing war activities on a truly grandiose scale. The same thing is going on in Germany, in France, in Japan, and everywhere. The period of an idyllic "peaceful" existence has sunk into Lethe; capitalist society is whirling in the mad hurricane of world wars.

It remains for us to say a few words about the future of class relations, since it is perfectly clear *a priori* that the new forms of capitalist relations cannot fail to be reflected in the situation of the various social groupings. The fundamental economic question is, What will be the fate of the various parts of the "national" income? In other words, the question consists in how the "national" product will be distributed among the various social classes, in the first place how the "share" of the working class will fare. We presume that the process is going on more or less alike in all the foremost countries, and that what is true for "national" economies is true for world economy.

A deep-going tendency towards decreasing real wages must be noted first of all. High prices resulting from the disparity of capitalist production not only will not become lower but, on the contrary, they will keep on rising (we have in mind prices that are distinct from specific "war time" dearth). The disparity between world industry and world agriculture will grow more and more, for we have entered an era of an accelerated industrialisation of agrarian countries. Growing militarisation and wars will immensely tighten the tax press, straining it to the utmost; "everything taxable will be taxed; everything taxed will bear the greatest possible tax burden" says a Russian trade paper.[1] And this is not an empty phrase. Where non-productive expenditures are colossal and the state budget is being reconstructed, increased direct and indirect taxation is inevitable. The mounting cost of living results also from other causes: first, prices are increased due to the increased tariff rates; second, there are monopoly prices in trustified industries; state monopolies in their turn will raise prices for fiscal reasons. The result will be that an ever greater part of the national product will be retained by the bourgeoisie and its state.

The opposite tendency, springing from the working class, will, on the other hand, be confronted with a growing resistance on the part of the consolidated and organised bourgeoisie that has grown to be one with the state. Workers' gains that were a usual phenomenon in the former epoch, become almost impossible. There takes place, not a relative, but also an *absolute* worsening of the situation of the working class. Class antagonisms become inevitably sharpened. This will take place also for another reason. State capitalist structure of society, besides worsening the economic conditions of the working class, makes the workers formally *bonded* to the imperialist state. In point of fact, employees of state enterprises even before the war were deprived of a number of most elementary rights, like the right to organise, to strike, etc. A railway or postoffice strike was considered almost an act of treason. The war has placed those categories of the proletariat under a still more oppressive bondage. With state capitalism making

[1] *Torgovo Promyshlennaya Gazeta*, 1915, No. 217.

nearly every line of production important for the state, with nearly all branches of production directly serving the interests of war, prohibitive legislation is extended to the entire field of economic activities. The workers are deprived of the freedom to move, the right to strike, the right to belong to the so-called "subversive" parties, the right to choose an enterprise, etc. They are transformed into bondsmen attached, not to the land, but to the plant. They become white slaves of the predatory imperialist state, which has absorbed into its body all productive life.

Thus the principles of class antagonisms reach a height that could not have been attained hitherto. Relations between classes become most clear, most lucid; the mythical conception of a "state elevated above classes" disappears from the peoples' consciousness, once the state becomes a direct entrepreneur and an organiser of production. Property relations, obscured by a number of intermediary links, now appear in their pristine nakedness. This being the situation of the working class in the intervals between wars, it will undoubtedly be still worse in war time. The *Economist*, the organ of the English financiers, was perfectly right when it wrote at the very beginning of the war that the world was entering an era of the most strenuous social conflicts.

CHAPTER XIV

World Economy and Proletarian Socialism

1. The capitalist and the worker as opposite poles of social relations. 2. Class antagonism of interests, and their relative solidarity. 3. Lasting interests and interests of the moment. 4. The so-called patriarchal relations between labour and capital. 5. The working class and the bourgeois state. 6. The working class and the imperialist politics of the bourgeois state (relative form of "solidarity"). 7. The working class and the war. 8. Collapse of "collaboration" with the bourgeois state, and regeneration of revolutionary Socialism.

THE first period of the war has brought about, not a crisis of capitalism (the germs of which were visible only to the most penetrating minds of both the bourgeois and proletarian camps), but a collapse of the "Socialist" International. This phenomenon, which many have attempted to explain by proceeding solely from the analysis of the internal relations in every country, cannot be more or less satisfactorily explained from this angle. For the collapse of the proletarian movement is a result of the unequal situation of the "state capitalist trusts" within the boundaries of *world* economy. Just as it is impossible to understand modern capitalism and its imperialist policy without analysing the tendencies of world capitalism, so the basic tendencies in the proletarian movement cannot be understood without analysing world capitalism.

Capital implies the existence of labour. Labour implies the existence of capital. The capitalist mode of production is a certain relation between people, between social classes, each of which implies the existence of the other. Viewed from this angle, both capitalists and workers are members, component parts, poles of the same capitalist society. In so far as capitalist society exists, there exists also an interdependence of these opposing classes, a mutual dependence, expressing itself in a relative solidarity of interests that are opposed in substance. This "solidarity" of interests is the solidarity of a moment, it is not that lasting solidarity which welds together the members of the same class. Bourgeois political economy, and together with it its "Socialist" followers, present that which is passing, momentary, accidental for the class struggle on a social scale as essential; they do not see the trees for the forest, and they inevitably sink to the rôle of simple satellites of finance capital.

Here is an example. Everybody knows that at the beginning of the capitalist era, when the working class had just begun to emerge and to separate itself from the small entrepreneurs, when so-called patriarchal relations prevailed between master and worker, the latter to a considerable degree identified his interests with the interests of his exploiter.

This identification of interests that are in substance totally opposed to one another, was, to be sure, not suspended in the air. It had a very real basis. "The better the business of *our* shop, the better for me," the worker of that time used to reason. This reasoning was based on the possibility of raising wages with the increase of the sum total of values realised by a given enterprise.

We find the same psychology in other variations. What, in fact, is, let us say, the so-called "craft ideology" of the English trade unionists? We find here substantially the same idea: *our* production, they say, *our* sphere of production, which embraces both workers and industrialists, must prosper before anything else. No interference of outside elements must be tolerated.

In recent times we find an analogy to this purely local patriotism in enterprises with highly skilled labour. Such enterprises, for instance, are the plants of the well-known American pacifist (and, incidentally, war contractor) Ford. The workers are carefully selected for the plant. They receive higher wages, they are granted various premiums and profit sharing under the condition that they be bound to the plant. As a result, the bamboozled workers are "devoted" to their masters.

On a larger scale the same phenomenon may be observed in the so-called working class protectionism with its policy of safeguarding "national industry," "national labour," etc. This ideology permeates a considerable part of the Australian and American workers: "We" (*i.e.*, both capitalists and workers), they say, are equally interested in *our* national industry, for, the higher the profits of our employers, the higher will our wages rise.

In the process of competitive struggle between the various enterprises, their situation is not everywhere the same. Enterprises with highly skilled labour always occupy the first ranks, always enjoy exceptional privileges. Their share in the surplus value that is being produced in society as a whole is disproportionately large, for they receive differential profits on the one hand, cartel rents (as far as we deal with modern times) on the other. Thus a basis is created for a momentary interlinking of the interests of capital and labour in a given production branch, a circumstance which expresses itself in the workers giving capital, not the labour of duty, but the labour of love.

It is perfectly obvious that such a "solidarity of interests" between the capitalist and the worker is of a temporary character, and (from the point of view of what "ought to be") it cannot determine the conduct of the proletariat. Were the workers eternally to hang on to the coat tails of their masters, they would never be able to conduct a single strike, and the employers, bribing them individually, would be able individually to defeat them.

However, because the proletariat has not learned yet to distinguish local and temporary interests from general and lasting ones, it is permeated with such a narrow conception. The latter is overcome only when the class struggle achieves great scope, destroying local bigotry, welding the workers together, and throwing them into sharp opposition as a class to the class of the capitalists. In this way the psychology of the patriarchal period was overcome when the bond of unity between the workers and the master of an individual enterprise was severed. In this way the "craft ideology" of the unions organising skilled workers was overcome.

However, the end of the nineteenth century, which to a large degree destroyed the bond of unity between capitalists and workers, which placed against each other those classes and their organisations as classes and organisations *hostile* to each other in principle, has not yet destroyed the bond of unity between the working class and the greatest organisation of the bourgeoisie, the capitalist state.

The working class connection with this organisation was expressed in the ideology of workers' patriotism ("social-patriotism"), in the idea of a "fatherland," which the working class is supposed to serve.

After what has been presented above, the material basis of this phenomenon will become clear if we turn our attention to the whole sphere of world economy.

We have seen that the competitive struggle was, by the end of the nineteenth and the beginning of the twentieth century, to a large extent transferred to the foreign markets, *i.e.*, it became a competition in the world market. Thus the state organisation of capital, the "fatherland," having turned into a state capitalist trust, took the place of the individual enterprise and appeared on the world arena with all its heavy and ponderous apparatus.

From this angle we must first of all view the *colonial policy* of the imperialist states.

There is an opinion current among many moderate internationalists to the effect that the colonial policy brings nothing but harm to the working class and that *therefore* it must be rejected. Hence the natural desire to prove that colonies yield no profit at all, that they represent a liability even from the point of view of the bourgeoisie, etc. Such a point of view is being propounded, for instance, by Kautsky.

The theory unfortunately suffers from one shortcoming, namely, it is out and out incorrect. The colonial policy yields a colossal income to the great powers, *i.e.*, to their ruling classes, to the "state capitalist trust." This is why the bourgeoisie pursues a colonial policy. This being the case, there is a possibility for raising the workers' wages at the expense of the exploited colonial savages and conquered peoples.

Such are exactly the results of the great powers' colonial policy. The bill for this policy is paid, not by the continental workers, and not by the workers of England, but by the little peoples of the colonies. It is in the colonies that all the blood and the filth, all the horror and the shame of capitalism, all the cynicism, greed and bestiality of modern democracy are concentrated. The European workers, considered from the point of view of the moment, are the winners, because they receive increments to their wages due to "industrial prosperity."

All the relative "prosperity" of the European-American industry was conditioned by nothing but the fact that a safety valve was opened in the form of colonial policy. In this way the exploitation of "third persons" (pre-capitalist producers) and colonial labour led to a rise in the wages of the European and American workers.

One highly important circumstance must here be noted: in their struggle for colonies, for sales markets, and markets for raw materials, for capital investment spheres, for cheap labour, not all the "state capitalist trusts" achieve an equal success. While England, Germany and the United States of America forged ahead in their triumphal march over the world market, Russia and Italy, all the strenuous efforts of the imperialists notwithstanding, proved too weak. It was in this way that a few great imperialist powers came to the forefront as pretenders to world monopoly. They have proved, as far as the others are concerned, "above competition."

Economically the situation is this. World surplus value is being divided in the struggle for the world market. As is the case within the framework of "national economy," so also within the boundaries of world economy, the stronger competitor (whose strength is increased by multifarious factors, like the structure of production, the strength of the state militarist apparatus, convenient location due to the presence of "natural monopolies," etc.) receives super-profits, a kind of differential profit (due to the superior structure of production) and a kind of cartel rent (due to the pressure of the militarist apparatus that fortifies monopolies).

Super-profits obtained by the imperialist state are accompanied by a rise in the wages of the respective strata of the working class, primarily the skilled workers.

Such a phenomenon could also be observed in olden times.

It was pointed out by Friedrich Engels who referred to the monopoly situation of England in the world market and to the conservatism of the English proletariat that resulted therefrom.

It was on the basis of this relative interest of the proletariat in colonial plunders that its connection with the masters' organisation of the bourgeois imperialist state grew and became strong. In Socialist literature this psychology found expression in the "national" point of view of the Social-Democratic opportunists. This "national wisdom," emphasised on every occasion, signified a complete abandonment of the point of view of revolutionary Marxism.

Marx and Engels viewed the state as an organisation of the ruling class that crushes the oppressed class with blood and iron. They assumed that future society would have no state at all, for the simple reason that there would be no classes. It is true that, for the transition period of proletarian dictatorship, when the proletariat is the temporary ruling class, they most correctly demanded a strong apparatus of working class state power to keep the overthrown classes in leash. Still, their attitude towards the oppressing state apparatus of the bourgeoisie was that of furious hatred, and from this point of view they mercilessly criticised the Lassalleans and other "statesmen." And a connection undoubtedly exists between this revolutionary point of view and the well-known thesis of the *Communist Manifesto* that the workers have no fatherland.

The Socialist epigones of Marxism have relegated this revolutionary opposition of Marx and Engels to the archives. In its place there emerge the theories of *"true* patriotism" and *"true* statesmanship," which, however, are in no way distinguishable from the most ordinary patriotism and the most ordinary statesmanship of the ruling bourgeoisie. Such an ideology was an organic outgrowth of the proletariat's partaking in the "great-nation policy" of the state capitalist trusts.

No wonder if after the outbreak of the great war, the working class of the foremost capitalist countries, chained to the chariot of the bourgeois state power, came to the aid of the latter. The proletariat was prepared for this by the whole preceding development; it was brought to this by its connection with the state organisation of finance capital.

However, the war itself, which could be waged only because the proletariat gave its tacit consent or showed insufficient indignation, has proven to it that its share in the imperialist policy is nothing compared with the wounds inflicted by the war.

It is in this way that there comes the crisis of imperialism and the rebirth of proletarian Socialism. Imperialism has turned its true face to the working class of Europe. Hitherto its barbarous, destructive, wasteful activities were almost entirely confined to the savages; now it thrusts itself upon the toilers of Europe with all the horrifying impact of a blood-thirsty elemental power let loose. The additional pennies received by the European workers from the colonial policy of imperialism—what do they count compared to millions of butchered workers, to billions devoured by the war, to the monstrous pressure of brazen militarism, to the vandalism of plundered productive forces, to high cost of living and starvation!

The war severs the last chain that binds the workers to the masters, their slavish submission to the imperialist state. The last limitation of the proletariat's philosophy is being overcome: its clinging to the narrowness of the national state, its patriotism. The interests of the moment, the temporary advantage accruing to it from the imperialist robberies and from its connections with the imperialist state, become of secondary importance compared with the lasting and general interests of the class as a whole, with the idea of a social revolution of the international proletariat which overthrows the dictatorship of finance capital with an armed hand, destroys its state apparatus and builds up a new power, a power of the workers against the bourgeoisie. In place of the idea of defending or extending the boundaries of the bourgeois state that bind the productive forces of world economy hand and foot, this power advances the slogan of *abolishing* state boundaries and merging all the peoples into one Socialist family. In this way the proletariat, after painful searching, succeeds in grasping its true interests that lead it through revolution to Socialism.

CHAPTER XV

CONCLUSION

History moves in contradictions. The skeleton of historic existence, the economic structure of society, also develops in contradictions. Forms eternally follow forms. Everything has only a passing being. The dynamic force of life creates the new over and over again—such is the law inherent in reality. Hegel's dialectics, which Marx placed on its feet, is valuable for this very reason that it grasps the dialectics of life, that it fearlessly analyses the present without being disturbed by the fact that every existence hides within itself the germ of its own destruction.

In its mystified form, dialectic became the fashion in Germany because it seemed to transfigure and to glorify the existing state of things. In its rational form it is a scandal and abomination to bourgeoisdom and its doctrinaire professors, because it includes in its comprehension an affirmative recognition of the existing state of things, at the same time also, the recognition of the negation of that state, of its inevitable breaking up; because it regards every historically developed social form as in fluid movement, and therefore takes into account its transient nature not less than its momentary existence; because it lets nothing impose upon it, and is in its essence critical and revolutionary in spirit.

Thus Marx in his foreword to the first volume of *Capital*. Many years have passed since; we already hear a new future knocking at history's door. Present-day society, which developing productive forces to a gigantic degree, while powerfully conquering ever new realms, while subjugating nature to man's domination on an unprecedented scale, begins to choke in the capitalist grip. Contradictions inherent in the very essence of capitalism, and appearing in an embryonic state at the beginning of its development, have grown, have widened their scope with every stage of capitalism; in the period of imperialism

168

they have reached proportions that cry to heaven. Productive forces in their present volume insistently demand new production relations. The capitalist shell must inevitably burst.

The epoch of finance capital has made all the elements of maladjustment of the capitalist organisation stand out in the boldest possible relief. In former times, when capitalism, as well as its class sponsor, the bourgeoisie, appeared as a progressive force, it was in a position partly to conceal its inner defects by comparing itself with the backwardness and maladaptation of pre-capitalist relations. Large-scale production, equipped with gigantic machines, ruthlessly crushed the handicrafts with their poor technique. This painful process was nothing but the collapse of pre-capitalist production forms. On the other hand, the very existence of those forms, of those various "third persons" in the capitalist production process, allowed capitalism to extend its power "peacefully," without exposing the limits put to economic evolution by its capitalist shell. This is why the general features of the contradictions inherent in capitalism as such, and forming its *"law,"* appeared in the sharpest possible form only at a stage of economic development when capitalism had outgrown its swaddling clothes, when it had not only become the prevailing form of the socio-economic life, but had even become the general form of economic relations, in other words, when it had appeared as world capitalism. It is only now that the inner contradictoriness of capitalism is expressed with dramatic force. The convulsions of the present-day capitalist world that is drenched in blood and is agonised in mortal pain, are the expression of those contradictions in the capitalist system, which in the long run will cause it to explode.

Capitalism has attempted to overcome its own anarchy by pressing it into the iron ring of state organisation. But having eliminated competition within the state, it let loose all the devils of a world scuffle.

Capitalism has attempted to tame the working class and to subdue social contradictions by decreasing the steam pressure through the aid of a colonial valve. But having accomplished this task for a moment, it thus prepared the explosion of the whole capitalist boiler.

Capitalism has attempted to adapt the development of productive forces to state limits of exploitation by resorting to imperialist conquests.   But it proved unable to solve that problem even through its own methods.

Capitalism has increased the power of militarism enormously.   It has brought to the historic arena millions of armed men.   The arms, however, begin to turn against capitalism itself.   The masses of the people, aroused to political life and originally tame and docile, raise their voices ever higher.   Steeled in battles forced upon them from above, accustomed to look into the face of death every minute, they begin to break the front of the imperialist war with the same fearlessness by turning it into civil war against the bourgeoisie. Thus capitalism, driving the concentration of production to extraordinary heights, and having created a centralised production apparatus, has therewith prepared the immense ranks of its own grave-diggers.   In the great clash of classes, the dictatorship of finance capital is being replaced by the dictatorship of the revolutionary proletariat.   "The hour of capitalist property has struck.   The expropriators are being expropriated."

THE END

INDEX

171

Made in the USA
Coppell, TX
11 December 2023

25847368R00098